www.rusi.org

Whitehall Paper 91

Making Mogadishu Safe: Localisation, Policing and Sustainable Security

Alice Hills

www.rusi.org

Royal United Services Institute for Defence and Security Studies

Making Mogadishu Safe: Localisation, Policing and Sustainable Security
First published 2018

Whitehall Papers series

Series Editor: Professor Malcolm Chalmers
Editor: Emma De Angelis

RUSI is a Registered Charity (No. 210639)
ISBN [978-1-138-32688-0]

Published on behalf of the Royal United Services Institute for Defence and Security Studies
by
Routledge Journals, an imprint of Taylor & Francis, 4 Park Square, Milton Park, Abingdon OX14 4RN

SUBSCRIPTIONS
Please send subscription order to:

USA/Canada: Taylor & Francis Inc., Journals Department, 325 Chestnut Street, 8th Floor, Philadelphia, PA 19106 USA

UK/Rest of World: Routledge Journals, T&F Customer Services, T&F Informa UK Ltd, Sheepen Place, Colchester, Essex, C03 0LP UK

Contents

About the Author

Alice Hills was professor of conflict studies at Durham University, 2013–2017. She is currently a visiting professor at the universities of Durham and Leeds, where her research is funded by the European Commission's Horizon 2020 research and innovation programme. Before joining Durham she was professor of conflict and security at the University of Leeds. Prior to that she taught defence studies at the UK's Joint Services Command and Staff College where she specialised in urban operations and police–military relations.

She has published widely on police development and on urban operations such as counterinsurgency and warfighting. Her publications include *Policing Africa: Internal Security and the Limits of Liberalization* (2000); *Future War in Cities: Rethinking a Liberal Dilemma* (2004); *Policing Post-Conflict Cities* (2009) as well as numerous articles in journals including *International Affairs*, the *British Journal of Criminology*, the *RUSI Journal* and *Stability*.

Preface

This book considers the best way to make the streets of a strategically significant and chronically insecure Southern city – in this case, Mogadishu – safe. It uses the city's neighbourhood-watch schemes to explore the ways in which Somalis, from politicians in the presidential compound of Villa Somalia to policemen and women street-sweepers in the rubbish-filled alleys of Waberi district, try to manage everyday security threats. Additionally, it considers the ways in which Somalia's international sponsors attempt to influence Mogadishu's security architecture and policing practices. Special attention is paid to the city's security plan and the points at which local and international interests meet.

The immediate challenges confronting the city are terrorism-related, but the legacy of 25 years of chronic insecurity means that threats are mutually reinforcing and reflect broader social and political tensions. It is difficult for me, as a non-Somali speaking white, European woman, to assess the full implications of this, let alone analyse accurately the personal strategies used by Mogadishu's inhabitants to stay out of harm's way. Nevertheless, exploring the city's security architecture and responses in this way provides contextual detail that offers insight into Somali policing priorities and the ways in which they interface with international practices. It also throws light on generic issues such as the nature of security and the security sector's contribution to state- and capacity-building.

The chapters that follow use the attempt by Mogadishu's Somali authorities to develop and implement an internationally acceptable security plan to discuss the relationship between counter-terrorism and softer forms of community safety, the contribution of community cohesion and mobilisation to sustainable policing provision, and the potential of information and communications technology (ICT) to improve the police–community engagement on which this is thought to depend. To explore the possibilities for generalising from Mogadishu's experience, the contribution of ICT to police–community relations in Hargeisa, capital of Somaliland, is compared.

Issues such as these are usually assessed in the light of the international community's high-level political agenda for the Federal Government of Somalia; May 2017's London Somalia conference on security governance and economic development is a case in point. But the emphasis here is on Somali perspectives on city and, more importantly, street-level security and police–community relations. The election of a new president in February 2017 may improve Mogadishu's security management, as may the allocation of billions of US dollars, euros, sterling, Turkish lira and Japanese yen to stability and development programmes, but to date new governments and aid projects have failed to improve neighbourhood security or community safety significantly, whereas the neighbourhood-watch schemes that this Whitehall Paper addresses have. Now is a good time to assess the prospects for making the city safer.

The research on which this paper is based received funding from the European Union's Horizon 2020 research and innovation programme under grant agreement No. 653909. But it would not have been achievable without the support and advice I received from international and Somali officials, officers and advisers in Mogadishu, Hargeisa and Nairobi, most of whom requested – or expected – anonymity. The views expressed are solely mine, but I am nevertheless indebted to the Somali Police Force, Benadir Regional Administration, African Union Mission in Somalia (AMISOM), European Union, United Nations Assistance Mission in Somalia (UNSOM), and, above all, to Stephen Fulcher and the security advisers working for an international consultancy based in Mogadishu without whose support my visit to the city would not have been possible. I am equally grateful to the Somaliland Ministry of Interior, Somaliland Police Force, and Transparency Solutions' Hargeisa office. Special thanks are due to the EU Capacity Building Mission in Somalia (EUCAP Somalia).

INTRODUCTION

Identifying the best way to manage everyday security in fragile post-conflict cities is as challenging today as it has ever been, and Mogadishu is one of the most challenging in the world, as the capital of the notoriously failed state of Somalia. This Whitehall Paper explores the ways in which Mogadishu's inhabitants try to stay out of harm's way, from security officials in the presidential compound of Villa Somalia to the city's powerful district commissioners, from patrolling policemen to the women road-sweepers in the rubbish-filled alleyways of the Waberi district. Its central proposition is that security is best understood as a coherent relationship or activity based on the need for physical safety today, rather than in the future. It uses the neighbourhood-watch schemes developed in certain districts of Mogadishu – most notably Waberi – to understand the ways in which the city's inhabitants respond to the security models promoted by international advisers, who in fact are based in the safety of the city's Aden Adde International Airport.

The most immediate security challenges confronting the city are terrorism-related, with the Islamic militant group Al-Shabaab the main concern, but the legacy of 25 years of conflict and violence means that the security threats faced by Mogadishu overlap with current terrorism and indeed are mutually reinforcing and indicative of broader political and social tensions. Special attention is paid in this paper to the city's security plan and the points at which the local and the international meet.

The level of insecurity in Mogadishu – and the length of time this insecurity has persisted – is extreme: at the time of writing, a truck bomb at a busy junction near key ministry buildings had killed at least 350 people, the country's deadliest attack.[1] Yet all sectors of society are exposed to a range of physical threats on a daily basis, arising from inter-clan conflicts, Al-Shabaab attacks, revenge killings, trigger-happy guards, or as a result of conflicts about land, property and livestock. Internally displaced persons (IDPs), members of minority clans and women are the

---

[1] *BBC News*, 'Mogadishu Truck Bombing Death Toll Jumps to 358', 20 October 2017.

1

most vulnerable. Further, the threat of physical insecurity is exacerbated by less tangible threats, with young Somali men between the ages of approximately 15 and 35 facing challenges that make them vulnerable to recruitment by Al-Shabaab.

The picture of insecurity in Somalia – and specifically in Mogadishu – presented in this paper is partial, reflecting the perspective of a non-Somali-speaking female British researcher who had only limited access to Somali residents. Nevertheless, by illustrating the responses and expectations of Somali inhabitants to the security challenges they face, this paper helps to rebalance a picture that is otherwise heavily weighted towards the concerns and perspectives of international organisations. In other words, it looks at how Somalis actually respond, rather than how they are expected to respond. In addition, the paper offers insights into larger issues, such as the nature of security and the contribution of police forces to state-building and capacity-building.

There is no shortage of reports analysing the innumerable security and humanitarian crises affecting Mogadishu since former President Siad Barre fled in 1991, ushering in more than two decades of civil war and insurgency.[2] But the establishment of the Federal Government of Somalia (FGS) in August 2012 saw a change of focus in news reports to emphasising Mogadishu's return to something approximating vibrancy: articles about property booms ran alongside stories about the installation of solar-powered street lights and photographs of residents going about their daily lives in markets, barber shops and restaurants.[3] The trend slowed in the run-up to the presidential elections in February 2017, with English-language Somali news sources such as *Shabelle News, Hiiraan Online, Horseed Media* and *Goobjoog News* publishing almost daily stories about Al-Shabaab's attacks, all of which continued in the weeks after the election. On 28 February, for example, in three separate incidents, a local government official and an intelligence officer were both killed by bombs hidden in their cars, while an army officer narrowly avoided

---

[2] For police-related developments in the early 1990s see, for example, Robert B Oakley, Michael J Dziedzic and Eliot M Goldberg (eds), *Policing the New World Disorder: Peace Operations and Public Security* (Washington, DC: National Defense University, 1998).

[3] Nazanine Moshiri, 'Mogadishu Property Boom Stirs Concern', *Al-Jazeera*, 14 October 2012; *Somalia Investor*, 'Real Estate Boom', 9 April 2016; Murad Shishani, 'Mogadishu's First Solar-Powered Street Lamps', *BBC News,* 29 October 2012; Mark Byrnes, 'A Fascinating Glimpse of Daily Life in Mogadishu', *CityLab*, 21 October 2013; *Keyd Media*, 'Somalia Resumes Solar-Powered Lampposts on Mogadishu Streets', 30 January 2015; Jason Burke, 'Three Tales of Mogadishu: Violence, a Booming Economy … and Now Famine', *The Guardian*, 15 May 2017.

assassination.[4] Nevertheless, most Somali and international commentators welcomed the election of President Mohamed Abdullahi 'Farmajo' Mohamed, a popular former prime minister who holds dual Somali-US citizenship. His election was widely thought to represent a genuine opportunity for Somalia to move towards stability, democracy and prosperity.[5] And everyone, including Farmajo, agrees that improving security – and developing the security forces – is a priority.[6] For physical security lies at the core of daily life.

Summary of Contents

Chapter I introduces the role played by Mogadishu's police and residents in the reconstructive efforts needed to stabilise, secure and, ultimately, develop the city. It explores the dynamics at play by linking three issues that are usually kept separate: hard and soft security as found in counterterrorism and community safety; formal and informal policing provision; and international and local perspectives on security. It argues that conventional distinctions between state-based security and individual or human security are misleading when making Mogadishu's residents safer requires physical security to be prioritised. The paper's central proposition – that security is best understood as a coherent relationship or activity based on the need for physical safety today, rather than in the future – is presented, together with its three key themes of counterterrorism, community policing and information and communications technology (ICT).

Chapter II introduces the reader to the city's security environment and the challenges it presents to local politicians, police officers and residents, as well as to donors such as the UK. It acknowledges the broad-based nature of its underlying insecurity but emphasises that the critical issue affecting decision-making and practice – and the one pulling together the various issues and acting as a concrete conceptualisation of insecurity – is terrorism. The ways in which the various elements relate are explored in the light of Mogadishu's formal city security plan and the role of the Somali Police Force. The overall picture is, however, complicated by Mogadishu's blend of formal and informal policing initiatives, the widespread acceptance of coercion in everyday life, memories of the

---

[4] *Shabelle News*, 'Somalia: A Local Govt Official Killed in Mogadishu Car Bomb Blast', 28 February 2017; Shamso Macalin, 'Bomb Under Car Seat Kills Somali Intelligence Officer', *Baydhabo Online*, 1 March 2017; *Shabelle News*, 'Top Army Officer Escapes an "Assassination Attempt"', 1 March 2017. Note: *Shabelle News* occasionally removes its online stories.

[5] Sakariye Cismaan, 'The Big Cheese: Why President Farmaajo Holds So Much Hope for Somalia', *African Arguments*, 9 February 2017.

[6] *Ibid.*

policing used during the 1970s and 1980s, and, most importantly, legal pluralism.

Chapter III focuses on the best example of a locally acceptable and sustainable form of community safety currently available in Mogadishu: the neighbourhood watch scheme found in Waberi district. The scheme's record is analysed in the light of the development of the 2015 Mogadishu city security plan, AMISOM's goal of rolling out community policing across the city's districts and, just as importantly, the Somali experience of security provision and policing in the 1970s and 2000s. It addresses the porous nature of the borders between not only counterterrorism and community safety and welfare, but also between state security forces, informal clan militias and terrorist groups such as Al-Shabaab, with some individuals belonging to all three. In Mogadishu, as in most chronically insecure cities, security reflects the sum of many local arrangements and is best explored by way of the points of interaction between the various actors and interests and the nature of the negotiations, concessions or refusals.

Chapter IV shows how, despite the neighbourhood-watch scheme's relative success, the relationship between Benadir's regional authorities, the police and residents is full of distrust and suspicion. Crimes ranging from property theft to violent assault potentially affect everyone, but most crime is not reported to the police and, even if it were, no-one expects officers to respond. Perhaps because of this, donors increasingly look to ICT as a tool for improving crime-reporting and police response rates. In some cases, ICT is seen as offering the potential for improving community cohesion, mobilisation and safety. Prompted by the success in Kenya of ICT-based reporting systems and the ease with which social media has been integrated into Kenyan community policing, and reinforced by the cheap call tariffs and high rates of access to mobiles in Mogadishu, donors have identified ICT as a tool for improving police–community relations and street-level security. Mogadishu's experience suggests that this is overly optimistic. Indeed, the chapter emphasises that Mogadishu's experience raises a number of important questions about the transferability of technology-based solutions between societies.

To explore the possibilities for generalising from a single case, Chapter V compares Mogadishu's experience of using ICT for community safety with Hargeisa's, where a text alert system was introduced in 2015. Although the project failed to achieve its goals, the alert system is noteworthy because it offers contextualised insights into both the specifics of police–community engagement in a relatively safe city and the use of mobiles as a two-way technology capable of reaching low-income or marginalised populations. It shows how, contrary to the Kenya-based debate mentioned in Chapter III, local norms and preferences can counteract the globalised technology available. The precise details of what shapes low-level policing in safe urban environments such as Hargeisa's may not be known, but ICT plays little part in its everyday policing practices.

The concluding chapter provides context-specific and generic observations addressing empirical and analytical concerns. Although the details of what Waberi's residents do to stay out of harm's way may not be fully known, three key points deserve note. First, neighbourhood-watch schemes represent the most locally acceptable, cost-effective and sustainable form of security currently available in Mogadishu. Second, counterterrorism and everyday safety concerns may be procedurally and financially separate, but they are not analytically exclusive. This suggests that while Western value-based divisions between security and development do not necessarily transfer to the Somali environment, the notion of a continuum based on everyone's need for physical security does. It indicates that donors should acknowledge that effective and realistic strategies for state- and capacity-building depend primarily on delivering physical security today, rather than 'human' security at some point in the future. Third, the potential of ICT to improve crime-reporting and police response rates is for now minimal in Mogadishu as in Hargeisa, because police stations are the preferred site for engagement.

I. MAKING MOGADISHU SAFER

The form of policing that the Federal Government of Somalia (FGS) is expected to develop has various ingredients. It is founded on the slippery terms 'security', 'state-building' and 'capacity-building' used by officials from intergovernmental organisations (INGOs), such as the UN and the EU, and other donors, including the UK. Academic commentators then refine these terms into notions such as 'traditional' or 'new' security in 'plural', 'twilight' or 'hybrid' states.[1] In addition, the form of policing to be developed by the FGS is expected to adhere to liberal values and ideals such as community, legitimacy, partnership, service, resilience and human security.[2] At the same time, it is required to address urgent challenges, such as rapid urbanisation, population growth, demographic change and violent extremism.[3] Yet, regardless of their functional or political focus, most such high-level discussions about security in Mogadishu emphasise the potentially critical role played by police forces in the reconstructive efforts to facilitate stability, security and, ultimately, development.[4] Whether this assessment is shared by Mogadishu's inhabitants is, however, questionable. Donors assume that the city's security officers, politicians, businessmen and residents wish to see the emergence of a functioning police force; but this may not be the case. In practice, little is known about the social and economic realities of Somali policing provision, and

---

[1] Joseph S Nye Jr, *Bound to Lead: The Changing Nature of American Power* (New York, NY: Basic Books, 1990); Christian Lund, 'Twilight Institutions: Public Authority and Local Politics in Africa', *Development and Change* (Vol. 37, No. 4, 2006); Roger Mac Ginty and Oliver Richmond, 'The Fallacy of Constructing Hybrid Political Orders: A Reappraisal of the Hybrid Turn in Peacebuilding', *International Peacekeeping* (Vol. 23, No. 2, 2016).

[2] See, for example, Roger Mac Ginty and Oliver Richmond, 'Myth or Reality: Opposing Views on the Liberal Peace and Post-war Reconstruction', *Global Society* (Vol. 21, No. 4, 2007).

[3] UN-Habitat, *World Cities Report 2016: Urbanization and Development: Emerging Futures* (Nairobi: UN-Habitat, 2016).

[4] OECD DAC, *OECD DAC Handbook on Security System Reform: Supporting Security and Justice* (Paris: OECD, 2007).

who benefits from the currently fragmented approach. This situation is unlikely to change in the foreseeable future: lack of security prevents researchers from conducting ethnographically informed fieldwork that might help to fill the knowledge gap, while the Somali 'cultural advisers' (often former diaspora) working for international organisations may pursue their own agenda.

In practice, relying on police forces to implement social or political changes according to the international community's agenda is inherently problematic.[5] Many recent conflicts and uprisings – from Afghanistan, Egypt and Iraq to Sierra Leone, Serbia and Syria – have been prompted or exacerbated by police brutality and corruption, and most police forces emerge tainted from conflict and rebellion. The same is true of societies experiencing political violence. Even in peacetime, the role of the police relies on the potential or actual use of coercion, and its orthodoxy is selective:[6] police forces reproduce the political and social order that those authorising or permitting their activities promote, while their officers are usually recruited from specific social strata or ethnic groups.[7] Additionally, police forces in regions such as sub-Saharan Africa, where many conflicts occur (South Sudan and Democratic Republic of the Congo, for example), are typically untrained, unpaid, under-resourced, and rely on physical coercion to achieve their goals, while their status is often lower than their military equivalents. All this ensures that they are distrusted by their political masters and other security forces, as well as by society.

Despite this, international policies for stabilising and developing post-conflict societies rely on donors promoting and supporting police reform projects that encourage police and local people to work together, and most draw on some form of community-oriented policing. Guidance for operationalising such approaches is drawn from ideas originally published in 2007 in the OECD's influential 'Handbook on Security System Reform',[8] and INGOs promoting broadly liberal approaches remain at the forefront of police reform projects. The EU, Somalia's biggest donor after the US,

---

[5] Alice Hills, *Policing Post-Conflict Cities* (London: Zed Books, 2009), pp. 54–57, 65–78; Otwin Marenin, 'Policing Change, Changing Police: Some Thematic Questions', in Otwin Marenin (ed.), *Policing Change, Changing Police: International Perspectives* (London: Routledge, 1995), pp. 3–22.

[6] Marenin, 'Policing Change, Changing Police'.

[7] *Ibid*.; Cynthia Enloe's work from the 1970s remains more relevant than donors might wish. See Cynthia H Enloe, 'Ethnicity and Militarization: Factors Shaping the Roles of Police in Third World Nations', *Studies in Comparative International Development* (Vol. 11, No. 3, 1976); Cynthia Enloe, *Police, Military and Ethnicity: Foundations of State Power* (New Brunswick, NJ: Transaction Books, 1980).

[8] OECD DAC, *OECD DAC Handbook on Security System Reform*.

the UK and Turkey, and its biggest funder of security reform,[9] invests millions of euros every year in the – broadly liberal – peacekeeping and police reform projects forming part of its Common Security and Defence Policy (CSDP) missions in, for example, Afghanistan, Kosovo and Bosnia-Herzegovina, as well as Somalia. The EU channelled $1.3 billion into Somalia between 2008 and 2017.[10] A large part of the EU's development funding to Somalia is financed by the European Development Fund, which since 2014 has committed $301 million to security and peacebuilding, food security, resilience and education in the country.[11] At the London Somalia Conference in May 2017, the EU pledged that its member states would invest $1.3 billion, bringing its total support to Somalia for 2017–20 to $4.5 billion.[12] However, although this figure includes police salaries, the EU (and the UN) has shied away from technical police training, preferring to support the African Union Mission in Somalia (AMISOM), development aid and humanitarian assistance. The EU, like most INGOs, addresses the least controversial aspects of police development, focusing on strategic or humanitarian issues, rather than the difficult-to-change and risky street-level security. Nevertheless, the EU regards the security and stability of post-conflict countries such as Somalia to be of great importance, affecting the security of its member states and its geopolitical interests. In practice, this means that the EU's interventions are driven by traditional security concerns, albeit leavened by 'softer', development-oriented goals that are presented in terms of the UN's Sustainable Development Goals, including gender equality and poverty alleviation.[13]

As with the EU, mixed interests are also evident in the security policy of influential bilateral donors such as the UK and the US. As the UK's then-Foreign Secretary Philip Hammond said on 2 June 2016 during a visit to Mogadishu, '[a] secure and stable Somalia is the UK's top priority in East

---

[9] For the OECD DAC's listing of official development assistance data for Somalia in 2014/15, see <https://public.tableau.com/views/OECDDACAidataglancebyrecipient_new/Recipients?:embed=y&:display_count=yes&:showTabs=y&:toolbar=no?&:show w>, accessed 9 June 2017; OECD, 'Aid at a Glance Charts: Somalia', <http://www.oecd.org/countries/somalia/aid-at-a-glance.htm>, accessed 9 June 2017.

[10] Fred Oluoch, 'EU Pledges More Support for New Somalia Government', *East African*, 6 March 2017.

[11] *Ibid.*; for humanitarian aid flows see Financial Tracking Service, 'Somalia 2017', <https://fts.unocha.org/countries/206/donors/2017?order=total_pledges&sort=desc>, accessed 31 July 2017.

[12] Fred Oluoch, 'Somalia Gets $1.3b for Economy, Security', *East African*, 16 May 2017.

[13] UN, 'Sustainable Development Goals', 2016, <https://sustainabledevelopment.un.org/?menu=1300>, accessed 17 December 2016.

Africa and is in our own national security interests'.[14] Driven by concerns about the influence of the Islamic militant group Al-Shabaab, which Hammond described as 'a terrorist organisation that cannot be allowed to take hold',[15] the UK's commitment to Somalia is evident from the £484 million sent in aid between 2009 and 2014.[16] Its current Somalia Security and Justice Programme has a budget of £32 million to provide the Somali Police Force (SPF) with basic training, infrastructure and skills in the two years to 2020,[17] and it remains committed to developmental objectives such as providing humanitarian assistance, overcoming poverty and inequality, and preventing conflict.[18] The UK's Department for International Development (DFID) also supports the re-establishment of basic policing in three urban areas 'liberated' from Al-Shabaab in south-central Somalia (Baidoa, Beledweyne and Kismayo) by assisting Somali authorities in recruiting up to 1,860 additional officers.[19] Additionally, the 2017 London Somalia Conference pledged $27 million to be spent on the training and mentoring needed to improve security over the next two years.[20]

Meanwhile, in March, General Thomas D Waldhauser, Commander of US Africa Command (AFRICOM), described Somalia as 'our most perplexing challenge'.[21] Yet the US's approach is shaped primarily by conventional security concerns, such as fears about Somalia representing a terrorist safe haven, or about Somali-Americans travelling to training camps in the Horn of Africa and conducting terrorist attacks on their return to the US. A small unit of US counterterrorism advisers was in Mogadishu in 2016–17 and

---

[14] Foreign and Commonwealth Office, 'Foreign Secretary Arrives in Somalia on Security Visit', press release, 2 June 2016.

[15] *Ibid.*; see also Home Office, 'Proscribed Terrorist Organisations', 29 September 2017, <https://www.gov.uk/government/uploads/system/uploads/attachment_data/file/578385/201612_Proscription.pdf>, accessed 5 January 2017.

[16] Alice Hills, 'Making Mogadishu Safe', *RUSI Journal* (Vol. 161, No. 6, 2016), p. 11.

[17] For details of UK aid, see Independent Commission for Aid Impact (ICAI), 'UK Aid in a Conflict-Affected Country: Reducing Conflict and Fragility in Somalia: A Performance Review', June 2017, <https://icai.independent.gov.uk/wp-content/uploads/EMBARGOED-Reducing-conflict-and-fragility-in-Somalia-ICAI-review.pdf>, accessed 30 June 2017.

[18] Jon Lunn, 'Somalia: February 2017 Update', Briefing Paper No. 7298, House of Commons Library, 16 February 2017, <www.researchbriefings.files.parliament.uk/documents/CBP-7298/CBP-7298.pdf>, accessed 4 March 2017; Department for International Development (DFID), 'DFID: Somalia', 2014, <https://www.gov.uk/government/world/organisations/dfid-somalia>, accessed 7 March 2017.

[19] UK Aid, 'Re-Establishing Basic Policing in Somalia [GB-1-204276]', 2017, <https://devtracker.dfid.gov.uk/projects/GB-1-204276>, accessed 7 March 2017.

[20] Oluoch, 'EU Pledges More Support for New Somalia Government'.

[21] Chege Mbitiru, 'Special Forces May Soon Join the War Against Al-Shabaab', *Daily Nation*, 5 March 2017.

soldiers from the 101st Airborne Division led a train-and-equip mission in 2017.[22]

To date, the results of the billions of euros, sterling and US dollars – and Turkish lira and Japanese yen[23] – spent on police-related reform and capacity-building have been uneven in Somalia. There are few – if any – cases in the world of externally driven fundamental organisational reform in police forces, let alone of value reform, whereas there are many instances of institutional resilience and individual resistance obstructing change: Afghanistan, Bosnia-Herzegovina, Kosovo and Sierra Leone remain fragile, and their police–community relations continue to be characterised by distrust and suspicion. Nevertheless, the absence of a realistic or politically acceptable alternative to managing instability and insecurity ensures the international community's continued commitment to reforming police provision, and thereby improving the police–community engagement thought necessary for stability and state-building. This is particularly testing in Mogadishu.

Somalia may no longer be routinely described as the world's 'most utterly failed state',[24] but it still topped the Failed States Index from 2008 until 2014, when it was replaced by South Sudan,[25] and its development is shaped fundamentally by its chronic insecurity. The effects of this are both negative

---

[22] Nick Turse, 'The War You've Never Heard Of', *Vice News*, 18 May 2017.

[23] Turkey has provided police training, although it forms only a small part of the 456 million liras ($121.9 million) of humanitarian aid given since 2011. See AMISOM Media Monitoring, 'Somalia Receives More than $121 Million in Turkish Aid', 10 March 2017, <http://somaliamediamonitoring.org/march-10-2017-morning-headlines/>, accessed 10 March 2017. Turkey has also established a $50 million base intended to support the Somali National Army (SNA). Turkish companies manage Mogadishu's Aden Adde International Airport and port, both of which are important sources of national (government) revenue, and at the time of writing it is seeking exclusive fishing rights off the coast of Somalia for eighteen years. See *Garowe Online*, 'Somalia: Turkey Aims to Win Exclusive Fishing Rights Off the Coast of Somalia', 10 May 2017, <http://www.garoweonline.com/en/news/somalia/somalia-turkey-aims-to-win-exclusive-fishing-rights-off-the-coast-of-somalia>, accessed 11 May 2017. Japan has for some years taken a leading role in developing the Somali and AMISOM police sectors by providing stipends for 5,000 Somali police officers, as well as the construction of police stations and the procurement of equipment, including armoured vehicles. See Permanent Mission of Japan to the United Nations, 'Statement by Tsuneo Nishida, Permanent Representative of Japan to the United Nations, at the Open Debate of the Security Council on the Situation in Somalia, 5 March 2012', <http://www.un.emb-japan.go.jp/statements/nishida030812.html>, accessed 15 September 2016. By 2012 its two trust funds had contributed a total of $38 million.

[24] *The Economist*, 'The World's Most Utterly Failed State', 2 October 2008.

[25] Somalia remains in second place. See Fund for Peace, 'Fragile States Index: Country Dashboard', <http://fundforpeace.org/fsi/country-data/>, accessed 7 June 2017.

and positive: terrorism, violent crime, corruption and clan-based conflict are rife, but so are entrepreneurialism, creativity, adaptability and social cohesion. Despite fragmentation, displacement and dysfunctional governance, the social fabric did not collapse after 1991 and Somalis looked – and continue to look – first to customary justice (including Sharia Law) and local or traditional non-state actors, such as elders, for solutions, rather than to 'state' representatives such as the police, who were either absent, ineffective or distrusted. Indeed, rather than asking why and for whom the Somali state is failing,[26] it is more realistic to ask why it is working at all (to borrow a phrase from Patrick Chabal and Jean-Pascal Daloz).[27]

This paper considers how, why and for whom Mogadishu works. Specifically, it addresses the best way to make the city's streets safer, but it takes the issue one stage further than most analyses by focusing on the interactions between formal and informal actors and processes, as well as between Somalis and donors. Further, it treats the city's security management as a single analytical field, rather than dividing it into separate categories. Its overarching analytical frame is that of the Mogadishu city security plan, the chief feature of which is counterterrorism. However, the focus of the paper is the Waberi district neighbourhood-watch scheme and what it tells us about the nature of the police–community engagement on which sustainable, state-based forms of urban security management and community safety are thought to depend. An additional issue is the potential of information and communications technology (ICT) to help prevent crime. The paper thus explores the links between three significant issues that are usually kept separate in scholarly debates:[28] 'hard' and 'soft' security as found in counterterrorism and community safety; formal and informal policing provision; and international and local perspectives on security. The emphasis throughout is on concrete conceptions of these issues and the insights they offer into Mogadishu's dynamics.

Key Themes

The best way to achieve cooperation between a police force and the inhabitants of post-conflict cities remains open to question, not least

---

[26] Morton Bøas and Kathleen Jennings, 'Insecurity and Development: The Rhetoric of the "Failed State"', *European Journal of Development Research* (Vol. 17, No. 3, 2005), p. 385.

[27] Patrick Chabal and Jean-Pascal Daloz, *Africa Works: Disorder as Political Instrument* (Oxford: James Currey, 2009); Alice Hills, 'Somalia Works: Police Development as State-building', *African Affairs* (Vol. 113, No. 450, 2014).

[28] See Jan Beek, et al. (eds), *Police in Africa: The Street Level View* (London: Hurst, 2017).

because the model of police and policing promoted by the OECD's 'Handbook on Security System Reform' was developed in and for industrialised Northern democracies.[29] Donors may emphasise the Somali police's potential to improve trust in the FGS, as well as its potential to help offset the influence of organisations that donors deem undesirable or illegitimate, ranging from clan militia to the National Intelligence and Security Agency (NISA).[30] However, the SPF plays little part in Mogadishu's day-to-day security, and even less in the territories outside the city. Nevertheless, its role is politically significant and is used here as an indicator of the orthodox international approach to policing provision that most of the city's residents, locals and internationals alike claim they would like.[31]

Two additional reasons support using this approach. First, unlike the Somali National Army's (SNA) predatory troops, who are based in barracks and live apart from local inhabitants,[32] the SPF's 4,463 registered officers[33] live and work in specific localities, and are familiar with their security environment and its dynamics – they would not otherwise survive. What they do or do not do is consequently informative, providing a realistic indicator of the nature of local security. So does the fact that informed international observers estimate the number of active officers to be approximately 1,200.[34]

Second, although the SPF in many ways does not fit into international categories, its role is analytically accessible because it shares certain functional and occupational commonalities with police across the world

---

[29] OECD DAC, *OECD DAC Handbook on Security Sector Reform: Supporting Security and Justice* (Paris: OECD, 2007).

[30] NISA is constitutionally illegitimate, but the FGS justifies its role in terms of the 1970 Decree 14 establishing President Siad Barre's National Security Service (NSS). Article 6 stated that members of the NSS could conduct arrests without a warrant; it was enough that they had been informed (or had a strong suspicion) that a crime had been committed against the state's security.

[31] See, for example, Observatory of Conflict and Violence Prevention (OCVP), 'Mogadishu 2014: Central Zone. Conflict and Security Assessment Report', 2015, <http://ocvp.org/docs/201407/Central%20Zone%20CSA.pdf>, accessed 28 January 2015; Hills, *Policing Post-Conflict Cities*.

[32] The number of SNA troops currently available is difficult to estimate. As *The Economist* notes, high rates of desertion, and soldiers' loyalty to clan leaders rather than the government, means that the SNA does not exist as a coherent force. See *The Economist*, 'Somalia: Most-Failed State', 10 September 2016.

[33] UN Security Council, 'Report of the Secretary-General on Somalia', S/2013/69, 31 January 2013, para. 28, <http://www.un.org/en/ga/search/view_doc.asp?symbol=S/2013/69>, accessed 4 April 2017. See also AMISOM's claim to have trained 6,000 officers over the course of its mission: 'AMISOM Police Newsletter', Jan–Mar 2017, p. 8.

[34] Author conversation with two international advisers, Mogadishu, 21 July 2016.

and is linked into international policing networks and organisations such as Interpol, which it joined in 1975. Further, donors and their technical advisers judge the SPF's development against two notable policing fashions: community policing and the emergent role of ICT. Both are assessed in light of counterterrorism, which dominates Mogadishu's security environment, or, to be more precise, responses to the threat posed by Al-Shabaab.

Counterterrorism
It is difficult to identify what constitutes an effective, realistic and locally appropriate strategy for dealing with terrorism in a dysfunctional city where terrorism reinforces, and is reinforced by, clan-based power politics, societal insecurity and violent crime. Indeed, many commentators argue that Somalia's insecurity reflects the attempts of key actors to access desirable resources such as business opportunities, political influence, and land and cash, rather than a power struggle between the FGS and Al-Shabaab.[35] It is equally difficult to say how any counterterrorism strategy should be used; in cities such as Mogadishu it invariably involves the application of hard security measures with covert military or paramilitary operations and physical coercion or extra-judicial killings. Donors and INGOs, such as the Djibouti-based eight-country trade bloc known as the Intergovernmental Authority on Development (IGAD), a major supporter of the FGS via AMISOM, may promote the use of softer preventative policies designed to address the underlying causes of violent extremism, but for now these have little traction in an environment where the focus is on short-term goals and where implementing a strategic approach is problematic. With the exception of the SPF's specialist bomb-disposal unit and NISA's Gaashaan units (a rapid-reaction counterterrorism force trained by US advisers), Somali forces lack the motivation, training, skills and resources needed to respond quickly and effectively to terrorist threats, and those units that are effective do not necessarily operate in a manner acceptable to the international community.[36] Significantly, this was not always the case; during the last two decades of Siad Barre's presidency, the SPF was notoriously effective, while a number of today's senior and mid-ranking officers were trained in countries such as the Soviet Union, China and Egypt.

Whether the reality of Somali policing is problematic as far as the Somali authorities are concerned is arguable, but it is classified as such by

---

[35] Alex de Waal, *The Real Politics of the Horn of Africa: Money, War and the Business of Power* (Cambridge: Polity Press, 2015).
[36] Jeremy Scahill, 'The CIA's Secret Sites in Somalia', *The Nation*, 10 December 2014.

the international organisations and advisers supporting them. Thus, on 22 February 2017, the UK's Foreign Office announced that it had hired GardaWorld, a Canadian security company, and Aktis Strategy, a UK consultancy, to improve the performance of Somalia's anti-terrorism units.[37] The next day saw advertisements for an instructor to train the SPF's 'hard arrest' Goodir Unit,

> to such a standard that they can conduct compliant independent day/ night detention operations in high threat areas, [are] fully competent in the recovery, preservation and continuity of evidence and become a sustainable capability within the Somalia Police Force and, in doing so, align this capacity building project with the wider policing work of British Embassy Mogadishu, and other donors.[38]

Community Policing
The second theme, community policing, is widely regarded by INGO and NGO bilateral donors as the most appropriate approach to policing, once security levels improve. Admittedly, the suitability of this approach to policing Mogadishu is debatable. Security may have improved, with overt and extensive conflict no longer taking place in the way it used to, but many international security managers working from Aden Adde International Airport argue that Mogadishu is not yet a post-conflict city.[39] More problematic is the fact that community policing is a controversial notion that is variously understood as: a philosophy that promotes and supports organisational strategies addressing the causes of crime; a problem-solving tactic; or a political label or descriptive term expressing an ideal of police–community partnership.[40] Further, the term reflects the liberal belief that police benefit from collaboration with local communities, which in turn profit from a more responsive police. The advocates of community policing assume that the police should provide 'services' that directly affect the life of communities, and that communities are the direct beneficiaries of police services. In fact, 'community' used in this context reflects a controversial political ideal. In this paper, it is understood as referring to the inhabitants or residents of a locality, who may or may not regard themselves as representing a coherent community.

---

[37] *Intelligence Online*, 'Training Somalia's Anti-Terrorism Units', 22 February 2017.
[38] Security Jobs, 'Experienced Training Mentor – Somalia', 23 January 2017, <http://internationalsecurityjobs.blogspot.co.uk/2017/01/experienced-training-mentor-somalia.html>, accessed 30 January 2017.
[39] Author conversations with security managers at Aden Adde International Airport.
[40] Mike Brogden and Preeti Nijhar, *Community Policing: National and International Models and Approaches* (Cullompton: Willan, 2005).

Regardless of whether coherent communities are a reality in Mogadishu, it is widely believed that a community-oriented approach to policing fosters the high degree of engagement needed to achieve a state of community security. When police engage with local communities and focus on community-based solutions to local concerns, the result is thought to be good-quality, responsive and accountable police services. From the perspective of donors, this approach to policing aims to re-establish broken links between communities and the police, create them where they may not have existed, or renegotiate them where necessary. It aims to change public perceptions of the police and rehabilitate police institutions in such a way as to encourage people to trust, interact with and support their police in preventing and reporting crime.

Information and Communications Technology
Community policing plays into a third theme, which is the potential of ICT (here ranging from computers and mobile phones to cartoons, posters and theatre) to improve police–community engagement. Perhaps because of the challenges of improving such relations and, more specifically, the trust on which they are thought to be built, there is a marked interest among donors in identifying, designing and developing context-specific solutions for improving crime-reporting and police response rates, and in their eyes ICT appears to offer what is required.

Donors assume that community involvement and support is needed if reform efforts are to have a chance of success, and mobile phones are increasingly seen as a tool capable of facilitating, strengthening or accelerating communication and information sharing between police and local people. This builds on the assumption of donors such as the UK that ICT 'plays a key and integrated role in accelerating progress' towards achieving politically desirable goals such as poverty reduction.[41] Meanwhile, the World Bank regularly presents ICT as a tool for improving service delivery and accountability in policing and other forms of community engagement.[42] And, despite the frequency with which reform projects are obstructed,[43] donors continue to believe that the development

---

[41] DFID, 'ICT for Development (ICT4D) Research and Capacity Development Programme', 2007–11, <http://r4d.dfid.gov.uk/Project/60422/>, accessed 4 October 2016.
[42] World Bank, 'Information and Communication Technologies', 2016, <http://www.worldbank.org/en/topic/ict/overview#1>, accessed 4 October 2016.
[43] See Alice Hills, 'The Dialectics of Police Reform in Nigeria', *Journal of Modern African Studies* (Vol. 46, No. 2, 2008), pp. 215–34; Alice Hills, 'Security Sector or Security Arena? The Evidence from Somalia', *International Peacekeeping* (Vol. 21, No. 2, 2014), pp. 165–80.

and maintenance of comprehensive and sustainable forms of peace and stability depends on trust-building between the police and the population. In turn, this is thought to depend as much on police showing an increased responsiveness to the population's needs as it is to police institutional reform, and ICT is thought to facilitate this.

This belief is understandable: recent years have seen the introduction in Africa of ICT for Development (ICT4D) and Mobile for Development (M4D), both of which have achieved some success in, for example, health provision.[44] Indeed, mobile-enabled services are increasingly seen as potentially transformational or, at the very least, as solutions that can facilitate service delivery when other types of traditional infrastructure are lacking, as they usually are in post-conflict environments in the Global South. Scaling up services and establishing sustainable business models is difficult,[45] as is using ICT for sensitive topics such as security, but the wide availability and perceived efficiency and effectiveness of ICT-based solutions only enhances their appeal. Regardless of local realities, the expectation among donors is that ICT-based solutions will help police relate to communities, ensure that local people are better informed and that police are held accountable, as well as improving police–community cooperation. From this perspective, ICT applications not only facilitate more efficient police services and improved access to police, but also mobilise citizens to fight crime and terrorism; they are thought to improve trust, accountability, police integrity and the community's ability to contribute to policing while personalising interactions.

There is much to be said for using ICT for policing purposes. Most people in sub-Saharan Africa have access to one or more mobile phones and, as the price and data costs of smart technologies continue to fall, donors are increasingly thinking of ICT as a potential solution to a range of communication and infrastructure problems. However, many countries struggle to maintain the power sources needed for basic mobile phones to work, let alone for more sophisticated technologies. Consequently, donors look to low-end mobile solutions, especially text messaging (SMS). Although SMS is a basic and relatively old technology, it is still commonly used and the wireless cellular infrastructure needed for this is relatively inexpensive. Given that mobile phones are the only two-way technology capable of reaching low-income and marginalised populations without access to proper infrastructure, it is not surprising that donors are looking to low-end mobile phones to improve social impact in policing provision. This is challenging in

---

[44] World Bank, 'ICTs for Health in Africa', 2012, <http://siteresources.worldbank. org/EXTINFORMATIONANDCOMMUNICATIONANDTECHNOLOGIES/Resources/ 282822-1346223280837/Health.pdf>, accessed 19 December 2016.

[45] GSMA Intelligence, 'Scaling Mobile for Development', 2013, p. 18.

fragile and violent post-conflict cities such as Mogadishu, but it is given urgency by the requirement for counterterrorism operations.

Balancing the Picture

It is difficult for international officials and analysts to accurately analyse Mogadishu's security dynamics. The threat of being kidnapped or harmed means that most never leave Aden Adde International Airport's fortified confines, which is run by Turkey's Favori airport management company and protected by AMISOM troops and commercial security companies staffed by European and South African contractors. It is arguably the most secure site in the country. Meanwhile, the complexity of the Somali language and the intricate nature of Mogadishu's clan-based society ensure that most international organisations and consultancies must rely on Somali cultural advisers (typically individuals who were formerly part of the Somali diaspora) for information and interpretation. This makes Mogadishu a good example of the gulf between international rhetoric and local realities found in most conflict-affected societies in the Global South. As a result, analysts do not have persuasive answers to seemingly straightforward questions: how does a non-functioning government facilitate the community mobilisation needed to manage terrorism, crime and insecurity in the absence of an effective police force? Can security agencies in failed or fragile states collect the intelligence needed for effective counterterrorism in a manner acceptable to rich and influential liberal democracies? If Mogadishu's government is as ineffectual as it appears, who has a city-wide overview of its security networks and environment, if anyone? How do the city's 1.4 million residents manage their everyday security needs?[46] Does the notion of community safety have meaning in a city as fragmented and violent as Mogadishu? Is the notion of community safety in Mogadishu fundamentally different to that in relatively safe cities such as Hargeisa, the capital of Somaliland? Does ICT have the potential to improve the police–community engagement on which sustainable policing provision arguably depends?

Most accounts of security in Mogadishu focus on the policy-relevant or strategic-level defence agendas of Somalia's international backers, including AMISOM, the US, the EU and Turkey,[47] or on technical projects to recruit

[46] World Population Review, 'Somalia Population 2017', <http://worldpopulationreview.com/countries/somalia-population/>, accessed 5 March 2017.
[47] For example, Paul Williams, 'Fighting for Peace in Somalia: AMISOM's Seven Strategic Challenges', *Journal of International Peacekeeping* (Vol. 117, No. 3–4, 2013).

and train more police, or on the activities of informal policing providers, such as the clan-based militia, whose widespread use is reinforced by the city's entrenched political economy and socio-cultural practices.[48] And there are persuasive reasons for assessing the situation in terms of either high-level international actors providing resources on which the FGS depends or low-level informal or community-based policing groups that provide the bulk of Africa's everyday security and justice.[49] Nevertheless, the resultant picture is unbalanced and incomplete as far as Mogadishu is concerned. In particular, treating the various strands of the picture presented so far in isolation fails to provide a realistic impression of today's nuanced situation, in which formal and informal providers interact, reinforcing each other's activities as often as they undermine them. It also ignores one of the more constructive insights emerging from the current situation, which is that Somalis appear to understand that the boundaries between different expressions of security (for example, counterterrorism and community safety) are more permeable than Western-based security studies acknowledge.

Several modifications are now in progress that may help to rebalance the overall picture and the role of police–community engagement within it. First, a strong academic trend is emerging which seeks to explain the societal dynamics associated with policing using concepts borrowed from anthropology and development studies, most notably bricolage, making use of what is available,[50] and hybridity, which alludes to the grafting of conventional state-based structures onto informal or clan-based forms of governance.[51] Ideally, the result is a more nuanced awareness of commonly used problem-solving approaches in Southern societies and what they tell us about people's understanding of security in the past, the present and the future. In particular, the ways in which Mogadishu's residents protect their property or family can provide insight into their understanding of the future.

Second, researchers are rediscovering the importance of the police for the populace in a diverse range of African countries.[52] In their comparison of

---

[48] See, for example, Ken Menkhaus, 'Non-State Security Providers and Political Formation in Somalis', CSG Papers No. 5, Centre for Security Governance, April 2016.

[49] Peter Albrecht and Helene Marie Kyed (eds), *Policing and the Politics of Order-Making* (London: Taylor & Francis, 2011).

[50] See, for example, Jean-Pierre Olivier de Sardan, *Anthropology and Development: Understanding Contemporary Social Change* (London: Zed Books, 2005); Albrecht and Kyed, *Policing and the Politics of Order-Making*.

[51] See, for example, Niagale Bagayoko, Eboe Hutchful and Robin Luckham, 'Hybrid Security Governance in Africa: Rethinking the Foundations of Security, Justice and Legitimate Public Authority', *Conflict, Security & Development* (Vol. 16, No. 1, 2016), pp. 1–32.

[52] Mirco Göpfert, 'Bureaucratic Aesthetics: Report Writing in the Nigérien Gendarmerie', *American Ethnologist* (Vol. 40, No. 2, May 2013); Sarah Biecker and

policing in Nigeria and South Africa, Sarah Jane Cooper-Knock and Oliver Owen found a high demand for police services even as officers fall short of expectations.[53] Indeed, they show how Nigerians and South Africans engage with police precisely because officers can perform valued bureaucratic tasks for them. Although the situation in relation to technically developed police forces such as Nigeria's is very different to Mogadishu, Cooper-Knock and Owen's insights raise questions about the ways in which a city's inhabitants use the police they often criticise. Mogadishu's experience reinforces this insight by showing how police, the authorities and residents share an understanding of their respective roles in managing low-level insecurity, which the donors may not like, but which locals find useful.

Third, the policy-relevant world is increasingly open to the potential offered by ICT, as are academic researchers.[54] A degree of police–community engagement is widely regarded by both internationals and local people as a key element in state- and capacity-building, but much depends on whether engagement can be improved by, for example, police becoming more accessible, more responsive or less corrupt. Better communications between police and local people are thought to be essential, although the projects for reforming police recruitment, training and working practices on which this arguably depends have to date made little fundamental difference to the way the police work or to the distrust with which local people regard them. Perhaps because of this, international organisations such as AMISOM and donors such as the UK Foreign Office look to ICT as a means of improving crime-reporting and/or police response rates in societies such as Mogadishu's, where there is widespread access to mobiles but also high levels of violence, crime and unemployment and low literacy rates. This paper specifically assesses the use of ICT as a tool for developing or enhancing the cooperation between

---

Klaus Schlichte, 'Between Governance and Domination – The Everyday Life of Uganda's Police Forces', in Lucy Koechlin and Till Förster (eds), *The Politics of Governance Actors and Articulations in Africa and Beyond* (London: Taylor & Francis, 2014); Sarah Jane Cooper-Knock and Oliver Owen, 'Between Vigilantism and Bureaucracy: Improving our Understanding of Police Work in Nigeria and South Africa', *Theoretical Criminology* (Vol. 19, No. 3, 2015).

[53] Cooper-Knock and Owen, 'Between Vigilantism and Bureaucracy: Improving our Understanding of Police Work in Nigeria and South Africa'.

[54] See, for example, University of Cambridge, 'New Communication Technologies and Citizen-Led Governance in Africa', pilot research project 2011–13, <http://www.cghr.polis.cam.ac.uk/research-themes/dmvp/NewCommsTech/CGHR_ICTsGovAfricaSummary.pdf>, accessed 9 April 2017; Edinburgh University Centre of African Studies, 'Social Media and Security in Africa', <http://www.cas.ed.ac.uk/research/grants_and_projects/sms_africa>, accessed 9 April 2017.

police and inhabitants that lies at the heart of notions such as community policing, because only then can it be understood how police and communities in fragile Southern societies develop and maintain locally acceptable working relationships.

Significance of Mogadishu for Exploring Police–Community Engagement

These issues are addressed here in the context of Mogadishu, arguably the most important city in the former Somalia. Cities, and Mogadishu in particular, are both the most fragile and resilient of political achievements and social relationships,[55] acting as sources of both insecurity and sanctuary. Consequently, Mogadishu offers a laboratory in which to explore the balance – in theory and in practice – between different types of security provision. In particular, it offers an opportunity to assess whether conventional distinctions between state-based security and individual or human security are misleading when – and this is the core hypothesis of this paper – both depend on the physical security of the residents of the society concerned. For physical security lies at the core of daily life.

The paper asks whether distinguishing between state and human security makes sense in Mogadishu, the capital of a state which has been variously described as failed, fragile, twilight, hybrid, or more precisely, an emergent state driven by informal or clan-based calculations. Does it make sense in a city in which all are vulnerable to acts of terrorism? Does it make sense to speak of state security when the politicians elected to state institutions are elected according to a clan-based 4.5 formula, one that gives equal quotas to the four major clans and a half-point to a cluster of minor clans who focus only on clan-based concerns?[56] Does it make sense to speak of human security when anecdotal evidence suggests that politicians care only about their own wellbeing, leaving the mass of the populace to focus on finding food, work and safety for today, rather than on equality and diversity tomorrow? The answer is that it does make sense to focus on food, work and safety for today rather than diversity

---

[55] Urban sociologists such as Georg Simmel and Louis Wirth captured this element of urban life by defining urbanism in terms of the density and diversity of human interaction and institutions, anonymity, and the breakdown of traditional community and its replacement by 'society'. See Gregory Andrusz, Michael Harloe and Ivan Szenyi (eds), *Cities After Socialism* (London: Wiley, 1996).

[56] Some Somalis include another clan in the power-sharing formula: Halane base at Aden Adde International Airport (that is, the international community). This makes it a 6, rather than 4.5 formula. See Oliver Chevreau, 'Federalism and Post-Conflict Statebuilding: The Case of Somalia', unpublished MPhil thesis, University of Bradford, 2017, p. 104.

tomorrow because these (and state-based security in particular) are the default standards against which Somalia is judged. Further, despite the literal and metaphorical fragmentation of cities such as Mogadishu, security is a coherent, comprehensive and relational concept founded on its inhabitants' need for physical security. This ensures that the security concerns traditionally associated with intelligence agencies interact with the counterterrorism tactics discussed at the presidential compound at Villa Somalia and the street-level safety approaches used in the city's districts to form part of a continuum based on physical security that blends into a broad-based and city-wide form of communal security.

These issues can be condensed into three empirical questions, each of which raises secondary queries:

1. What is the most cost-effective, sustainable and locally acceptable way to collect the information and actionable intelligence needed to make Mogadishu's residents safe?
    ○ How is security-related knowledge produced, authenticated, ordered and articulated, and how are gaps and uncertainties managed?
    ○ How does the collection of intelligence relate to residents' individual and group security strategies?
    ○ In what circumstances are existing approaches and knowledge adapted in anticipation of the future?
2. What is known about the relationship between counterterrorism and community safety and welfare in a city such as Mogadishu?
    ○ How, where and why does counterterrorism interact with community safety?
    ○ Where are the tipping points between security, stability and development?
    ○ Can concrete problem-solving actions help to generate new insights?
3. To what extent can ICT help to improve the police–community engagement on which stable and sustainable forms of low-level urban security depend?
    ○ Can ICT improve crime-reporting and/or police response rates?
    ○ How might the use of ICT, surveillance and data availability influence and shape the location, demands and results of police–community engagement?
    ○ Is Mogadishu's experience fundamentally different to that of safer Somali cities such as Hargeisa?

To investigate these questions, this paper draws on analyses conducted in Somaliland, Puntland and Mogadishu in 2011, 2015 and 2016. Earlier work carried out by the author for the UN Development Programme (UNDP) in Somaliland and Puntland addressed the relationship between police development, structural conditions and political events rather than police–community engagement as such, but it provided insight into the relationship between Somali police forces, political authorities and communities in urban areas. This was supplemented by EU-supported research in Hargeisa in Somaliland in December 2015 and March 2016, which used residents' attitudes to the application of ICT for crime prevention to analyse police–community relations. From 2011 to 2015, interviews with Somali police officers, officials and NGO activists in Mogadishu were conducted by telephone from or in Nairobi, although most of the research used here was carried out in person in Mogadishu in July 2016. Inevitably, access to the city's residents, police and politicians was limited. This meant that much of the information came from international advisers and trainers who were based at Aden Adde International Airport but worked in the city, former diaspora living and working in nearby districts, and Somali NGO representatives able to access the airport's periphery, as well as AMISOM and UN officers and officials confined to the airport. The risk of the assessment being over-reliant on the policies and agenda of international organisations was partly offset by the willingness of many internationals to speak frankly (and off the record) about the realities of working with Somali officials, police officers and inhabitants. It was also balanced by insights from the broader literature on the occupational commonalities shared by police around the world,[57] by earlier work completed by the author on police reform and policing practices in volatile Muslim cities,[58] and by closely monitoring Somali news sites such as *Shabelle News* and *Garowe Online*, as well as AMISOM's twice-daily media reports.[59]

Admittedly, this approach raises questions not only about bias but also about how qualitative similarities emerge from different cases, places and years. Are comparisons between Mogadishu and Hargeisa possible? Are any coincidences or common principles at work? What are the recurring

---

[57] Alice Hills, 'What is Policeness? On being Police in Somalia', *British Journal of Criminology* (Vol. 54, No. 5, 2014), pp. 765–83; Jana Hönke and Markus-Michael Müller (eds), *The Global Making of Policing: Postcolonial Perspecticves* (London: Routledge, 2016).

[58] For example, Alice Hills, 'Lost in Translation: Why Nigerian Police Don't Implement Democratic Reforms', *International Affairs* (Vol. 88, No. 4, 2012); Alice Hills, 'Policing a Plurality of Worlds: The Nigeria Police in Metropolitan Kano', *African Affairs* (Vol. 111, No. 442, 2012).

[59] AMISOM's monitoring reports act as a safety filter for items from potentially dangerous sources. Internet resources are invaluable, but they are also fluid and some pages from, for example, *Shabelle News* are no longer available.

elements? How are potential irregularities and patterns best identified? Nevertheless, the approach narrows down otherwise overly broad ideas of security-related beliefs and practices, providing analytical focus. It also helps provide a context for what might otherwise be trivial generalisations 'valid only under certain conditions',[60] while suggesting that similar response patterns are identifiable across the Somali entities. The meaning of terms such as 'danger', 'security' and 'protection' are not self-evident or necessarily observable, so exploring them in the context of Mogadishu and Hargeisa helps to identify potential commonalities.

---

[60] Nicos Mouzelis, *Modern and Postmodern Social Theory* (Cambridge: CUP, 2008), p. 19.

II. POLICING MOGADISHU

At first glance, Mogadishu's security governance is organised conventionally. The coastal city was formally recognised as the capital of the federal republic when the internationally acknowledged FGS was established in 2012, and it hosts Somalia's parliament, supreme court, prime minister's office and the presidential palace, known as Villa Somalia. Located in Benadir region, it also acts as the capital of the Benadir Regional Administration (BRA) which, headed by the mayor of Mogadishu, covers the same area as the city and plays a significant role in the politics and decision-making of its seventeen districts (it receives 15 per cent of the federal budget).[1] Benadir is the smallest administrative region in Somalia, but has the largest population, which in 2014 the UN estimated as approximately 1.65 million.[2] This figure includes approximately 369,000 IDPs.

Mogadishu's security is officially managed by the SPF and less officially by NISA and its military counterterrorism force, Gaashaan ('Shield'), essentially the regional administration's intelligence agency.[3] The Somali National Army is not operating formally in Mogadishu, its head having agreed in March 2017 to pull all military personnel from the city (4,000 had been present, most of whom had not been paid for months[4]).[5] However, this situation may yet change as a result of three decisions taken in April and May 2017.

---

[1] UN Office for the Coordination of Humanitarian Affairs, 'Benadir Region: Mogadishu City', 2012, <http://reliefweb.int/sites/reliefweb.int/files/resources/120316_Administrative_Map_Banadir_A4.pdf>, accessed 9 April 2017.

[2] United Nations Population Fund, 'Population Estimation Survey 2014 for the 18 Pre-War Regions of Somalia', October 2014, p. 31, <https://reliefweb.int/sites/reliefweb.int/files/resources/Population-Estimation-Survey-of-Somalia-PESS-2013-2014.pdf>, accessed 12 January 2018.

[3] Puntland, Somaliland, Jubaland and South West State have their own intelligence agencies.

[4] Personal communication with author.

[5] *Garowe Online*, 'Somali President Meets with Army Chiefs to Address Insecurity', 7 March 2017, <http://www.garoweonline.com/en/news/somalia/somali-president-

First, in April 2017 the FGS and parliament endorsed proposals for a new countrywide framework that could affect Mogadishu's security architecture, under which Somalia will have: a 22,000-strong defence force, while its police will consist of 32,000 officers divided into six units in line with pre-1991 arrangements; a paramilitary unit (Darwish); a tax protection unit; diplomatic guards; a Criminal Investigations Department (CID); and a coast guard (there is no mention of a general duties police).[6] A new National Security Council representing the federal states will determine the management of internal security threats.

Second, a stabilisation force was created with a remit to target illegal firearms, Al-Shabaab members and militia groups claiming to be government soldiers, all of which was intended to protect the city during Ramadan (26 May–24 June 2017), when terrorist attacks increase in frequency. Third, in early May, President Farmajo's newly appointed governor of Benadir and mayor of Mogadishu – a 35-year-old former diplomat[7] – announced that the regional administration's security committee, created in 2013, would be replaced with a new regional-level security committee.[8] These developments were followed by a flurry of initiatives that included an announcement in July that a special force would be created to guard government installations and officials. This force would replace NISA, which would revert to 'plain clothes' duties.[9] Yet a fundamental change to policing is unlikely because the FGS is determined to prevent the regional administration from achieving the autonomy that might herald significant

meets-with-army-chiefs-to-address-insecurity>, accessed 7 March 2017. Many soldiers are experienced but undisciplined fighters. As the humanitarian news agency IRIN noted in 2013, 'Somalia's armed forces comprise some 20,000 soldiers, defined as those fighting Al-Shabab [sic], including militias not formally integrated into the military. Around 13,000 soldiers receive regular financial payments, most of which are paid by the international community'. See IRIN, 'Somali Security Sector Reform', 13 May 2013, <https://www.irinnews.org/fr/node/253499>, accessed 24 May 2013. This prompted a senior diplomat to observe that, '[N]ever has so much been invested in so many and turned into so few'. John Aglionby, 'Somalia's President Mohamed Takes Power in Fragile State', *Financial Times*, 10 February 2017. See also Menkhaus, 'Non-State Security Providers and Political Formation in Somalia', p. 23. On 18 May, several hundred soldiers mutinied over unpaid wages, although they soon returned to their barracks.
[6] *AMISOM Daily Media Monitoring*, 'Parliament Approves Security Architecture with Few Amends', 3 May 2017, <http://somaliamediamonitoring.org/may-3-2017-morning-headlines/>, accessed 3 May 2017.
[7] Judy Maina, 'Somali President Appoints New Mogadishu Mayor with High Hopes for Change', *AllEastAfrica*, 6 April 2017.
[8] *Somali Update*, 'Somalia: To Ease Pressure, Mogadishu Mayor Appoints New Security Committee', 9 May 2017.
[9] *Horn Observer*, 'Somali Government to Form Special Forces in Charge of the Security Officials and Government Offices – Minister', 18 July 2017.

modification. For example, in January 2018, Farmajo sacked the mayor on the basis that the latter wanted Mogadishu to become equal to Somalia's six regional states, each of which has its own president.[10] Change is further obstructed by the Somali preference for clan-based selection,[11] informal decision-making, tactical flexibility,[12] and for settling slights and disputes with guns.[13] Arguably, innovation and fundamental disruption to current practices, seen as desirable by some international donors, are not in the interests of the international advisers and trainers supporting the security forces either, as too much would depend on the coercive effectiveness of, for example, Gaashaan's Alpha and Bravo components, which are trained in urban operations by US and international advisers, as is a separate NISA commando unit, Danab ('Lightning').

But appearances are deceptive. Donors may describe Mogadishu's governance structures in conventional terms, but the reality is anything but conventional: the FGS barely functions; mayoral politics pursues its own agenda; many police and military units are infiltrated by militia or Al-Shabaab sympathisers; much of the fighting and policing that takes place is carried out by clan-based militia and paramilitaries; and the government has so far lacked the political will and capacity to address this. The 2017 London Somalia Conference may have referred to a 'fair and equitable' distribution of the Darwish paramilitary policing unit between federal and state-level police, together with 'strong civilian oversight' and the involvement of civil society organisations in police development,[14] but this means little when politicians are concerned only to recoup the often substantial costs of their appointment, when powerful clan interests are at

---

[10] *Shabelle News*, 'Somalia Deploys Forces in Mogadishu after President Fires Mayor', 21 January 2018.

[11] Some members of the National Security Council argue that the new army (in other words, national security) should be based on the 4.5 power-sharing formula. See *AMISOM Daily Media Monitoring*, 'Challenges Emerge at the National Security Council Meeting', 7 July 2017.

[12] For an informative discussion, see the rationale for swarm tactics described in David Kilcullen, *Out of the Mountains: The Coming Age of the Urban Guerrilla* (London: Hurst, 2013), pp. 80–86.

[13] For example, in May 2017, guards from the SNA and NISA exchanged fire outside the Benadir administration's headquarters when a NISA convoy was stopped at a security checkpoint. *AMISOM Daily Media Monitoring*, 'Gunfire Exchange Between Villa Somalia Guards and NISA Benadir Boss Leaves Two Dead', 17 May 2017. In July, four soldiers, including the former head of Benadir intelligence, were killed by NISA in a clash near Villa Somalia. See *Shabelle News*, 'Former Intelligence Officer Among 4 Killed in Mogadishu Fighting', 26 July 2017.

[14] London Conference Somalia, 'Security Pact', 11 May 2017, pp. 6, 9, <https://www.gov.uk/government/uploads/system/uploads/attachment_data/file/613720/london-somalia-conference-2017-security-pact.pdf>, accessed 15 May 2017.

play, when security forces are not paid regularly, when ministries do not operate as institutions, and when the capacity of district administrations is low.[15] It is not by accident that Transparency International repeatedly identifies Somalia as the most corrupt country in the world.[16] In Somalia there are no formal judicial or taxation structures, nor are there regulations covering foreign investment, and in 2016 the government's debts were approximately $5 billion, whereas revenues (mainly from airport fees) were approximately $230 million.[17] Donors such as the UK repeatedly promote financial accountability and professionalism whilst providing the police with training in human rights, leadership, management and investigative skills, but neither politicians nor the security sector answer to the formal civilian authorities.[18] Meanwhile, the approximately 7,000–9,000 fighters belonging to the militant Islamist group Al-Shabaab capitalise on the government's inability to provide street-level security.[19] For example, just a few days after Farmajo's election, Al-Shabaab paraded 800 new fighters in the southern town of Jilib, promising to continue its decade-long war.[20]

In practice, Mogadishu's style of governance reflects a preference for opaque decision-making and tactical flexibility. Regardless of Farmajo's election, it reflects an environment in which Somali politicians and power brokers think in terms of clan interests, government authorities are unresponsive to people's needs, and social factors play out in the political sphere.[21] Consequently, with the exception of a handful of activists,

---

[15] Abdikahim Ainte, 'Can the Credibility of Somalia's Indirect Elections be Salvaged?', *African Arguments*, 5 January 2017; *Waagacusub*, 'President Sacks HabarGidir Officials and Replaces to his Clansmen', 19 March 2015; De Waal, *The Real Politics of the Horn of Africa*.

[16] Transparency International, 'Corruption Perceptions Index 2016', 2017, <http://www.transparency.org/whatwedo/publication/corruption_perceptions_index_2016>, accessed 9 April 2017.

[17] Aglionby, 'Somalia's President Mohamed Takes Power in Fragile State'. Hence the international community's welcome of the Communications Act of September 2017, which aims to regulate a sector that the World Bank estimates could potentially contribute up to 11 per cent of Somalia's GDP. See World Bank, 'Legal ICT Framework is Pivotal Moment for Somalia', 2 October 2017.

[18] 'Arena' is a more accurate description. See Alice Hills, 'Security Sector or Security Arena? The Evidence from Somalia', *International Peacekeeping* (Vol. 21, No. 2, 2014).

[19] Council on Foreign Relations, 'Al-Shabab in Somalia', 22 February 2017, <http://www.cfr.org/global/global-conflict-tracker/p32137#!/conflict/al-shabab-in-somalia>, accessed 7 March 2017.

[20] *Shabelle News*, 'Al Shabaab Vows to Fight New Somali Government', 13 February 2017.

[21] Yann-Cédric Quero, Mireille Widmer and Lindsey Peterson, *Safety and Security: Mogadishu* (Hargeisa: Observatory of Conflict Violence and Prevention, 2011), p. 36.

Observatory of Conflict and Violence Resolution (OCVP) workers and diaspora researchers, no-one asks the residents of districts such as Waberi what they need or want.[22] This results in high levels of suspicion on all sides, which undermine support for the international community's capacity-building projects, such as police reform. For Mogadishu's Somali inhabitants, physical safety and survival are more pressing concerns than appointing national security committees or developing institutions, financial accountability procedures or rights-based policing. And the views of focus groups conducted in the districts by OCVP in 2011 remain valid: there is a 'lack of faith in the ability of the community (let alone the state) to protect individuals, a sense of injustice, trauma, and general hopelessness for the future'.[23]

Parallel Initiatives

The overarching challenge confronting Mogadishu's inhabitants in 2017, just as it was in 2007 and 1997, is insecurity. The state is absent, and residents remain dependent on informal neighbourhood and clan-based groups for protection and policing. Indeed, clan-based commitments and obligations are the only guarantees most inhabitants can rely on; everything depends on clan or personal relationships filtered through clan affiliation, rather than on government directives or institutions.[24] Although little may be known about the ways people try to minimise their exposure to harm, it is clear that they must fend for themselves in the face of high rates of theft, kidnapping (especially for ransom), sexual violence and gun-related murders, which many see as components of broader conflict dynamics, rather than as separate events.[25]

---

[22] See, for example, the work of Abdulhakim Mohamed Hadi, director of Somali Neighborhood Organization (SONO) and Benadir's former director of communities; see *Amisom Daily Media Monitoring*, 'Neighbourhood Watch Director Resolute in Restoring Safety In Mogadishu', 13 July 2015; Quero, Widmer and Peterson, *Safety and Security*; Egal, 'Police Corruption, Radicalization and Terrorist Attacks in Mogadishu', pp. 27–30.

[23] Quero, Widmer and Peterson, *Safety and Security*; see also Robert Young Pelton, Mohamed Nuxurkey and Suleiman Osman, 'The Police of Somalia, Somaliland, Puntland', SomaliaReport, 31 May 2012, p. 28, <http://piracyreport.com/index.php/post/3402/The_Police_of_Somalia_Somaliland_Puntland_>, accessed 1 June 2012.

[24] Virginia Luling, 'Genealogy as Theory, Genealogy as Tool: Aspects of Somali "Clanship"', *Social Identities* (Vol. 12, No. 4, 2006); Joakim Gundel, 'Clans in Somalia: Report on a Lecture by Joakim Gundel, COI Workshop, Vienna, 15 May 2009 (Revised Edition)', 15 December 2009, Austrian Red Cross, Vienna, <http://www.ecoi.net/file_upload/90_1261130976_accord-report-clans-in-somaliarevised-edition-20091215.pdf>.

[25] Quero, Widmer and Peterson, *Safety and Security*, p. 21.

Admittedly, the city is less dangerous than it used to be: in 2016 there were fewer clan-based conflicts and anecdotal evidence suggests that people feel safer as a result. However, new sources of insecurity have emerged, increasing uncertainty and encouraging new tensions:[26] suicide attacks, truck bombs, grenade attacks, targeted killings and land disputes exacerbate long-standing fears about personal safety and violent crime. There are few, if any, reliable statistics, but in 2015 OCVP reported that young men in the relatively safe central districts were particularly concerned about terrorism, while women feared clan-based conflict, and both attributed violence to easy access to guns, chewing the mild narcotic khat, and unemployment.[27] Somalia receives weapons from Eritrea, Ethiopia, Djibouti, Libya, Iran, Saudi Arabia, Ukraine, the US and Yemen, and it is thought that more AK-47s, rocket launchers, mines and machine guns are in circulation now than during the 2000s.[28] This situation helps to explain why disarmament is not necessarily welcomed, least of all by the city's armed politicians.[29] The result is that physical security remains the fundamental need – everyone wants personal safety and the safety of their property today, rather than access to health or education provision at some point in the future. How, then, can the realities of the city's security governance and provision best be understood? What are its implications for understanding security more broadly?

The most significant feature to note about Mogadishu's security environment is that security provision operates across a number of levels, which nevertheless comprise one field. Formal and informal actors and provision interact, individuals move between security forces,[30] the borders

---

[26] Heritage Institute for Policy Studies, 'Perceptions of Security and Justice in Mogadishu Interpreting Results of the OCVP Conflict and Security Assessment', 2014, p. 1.

[27] OCVP, 'Mogadishu 2014: Central Zone – Conflict and Security Assessment Report', p. 11, <http://ocvp.org/docs/201407/Central%20Zone%20CSA.pdf>, accessed 3 February 2016. For further discussion about khat see, for example, James Jeffrey, 'Khat in the Horn of Africa: A Scourge or Blessing?', *Inter Press Service*, 12 March 2017, <http://www.ipsnews.net/2017/03/khat-in-the-horn-of-africa-a-scourge-or-blessing/>, accessed 10 May 2017.

[28] *Indian Ocean Newsletter*, 'Gulf of Aden, Arms Supermarket', 1 April 2016.

[29] *AllAfrica*, 'Nisa Chief Issues Tough Warning to Armed Mogadishu Politicians Over Disarmament Exercise', 13 June 2017.

[30] For example, Mohamed Aden Jimale (Koofe) was appointed Director of Immigration and the Civil Aviation Agency in July 2016, but he was formerly Head of Operations for Benadir's NISA office and, reputedly, a member of Al-Shabaab. See *Indian Ocean Newsletter*, 'Former Shabaab Member Named Immigration Director', 29 July 2016.

between 'hard' and 'soft' security blur,[31] and Somali authorities exploit, accommodate, mimic, undermine or ignore the processes, ideals and values promoted by their international sponsors.[32] Meanwhile, anecdotal evidence collected during the research for this paper suggests that the city's residents accommodate this situation and do not find it problematic; they tolerate ambiguities, choosing their providers and reporting channels according to the circumstances in which they find themselves. Additionally, their choice is influenced by the knowledge that they cannot rely on assistance from government representatives, such as the SPF and NISA or, for that matter, AMISOM. Indeed, the presence of AMISOM's troops and formed police units is considered by many to be divisive and in some cases dangerous. It is probable that the views of today's residents differ little from those of OCVP's respondents in 2014. AMISOM helps to keep the peace, but its motives are questioned: there is a widespread perception among residents that it prolongs its presence in order to collect international resources.[33]

Residents' choices are also affected by the members of the formal security forces demonstrating ill-discipline, and a lack of coordination, as well as the perception that they have been infiltrated by Al-Shabaab sympathisers.[34] There is confusion over the forces' respective roles, which is not helped by police officers being described as 'soldier-policemen', NISA troops being called 'detectives', taxmen being referred to as 'policemen', and militia and criminals wearing police uniforms. Indeed, some of the respondents to OCVP's 2014 survey said that some police, in particular, acted like clan militias in uniform.[35] But, in practice, residents accommodate the fact that police performance is hindered by pay arrears, inadequate equipment and poor training by looking to elders or militia groups for security. Most of OCVP's respondents said they would prefer to report serious crime to the police, rather than to elders (and anecdotal evidence from Waberi district suggests that some neighbourhoods have a good working relationship with their police commander), but this is not practical because the police release suspects as soon as their relatives pay a suitable bribe.

In this way, formal schemes intersect with informal initiatives and traditional and militia-based groups.[36] Indeed, in many districts militias are

---

[31] Soft power refers to the ability to persuade, rather than coerce. See Joseph S Nye Jr, *Soft Power: The Means to Success in World Politics* (New York, NY: Public Affairs, 2004).
[32] Hills, 'Somalia Works', p. 103.
[33] OCVP, 'Mogadishu 2014', p. 16.
[34] *Ibid.*, pp. vii, viii.
[35] *Ibid.*, p. 16.
[36] See, for example, Peter Albrecht and Louise Wiuff Moe, 'The Simultaneity of Authority in Hybrid Orders', *Peacekeeping* (Vol. 3, No. 1, 2015).

the only reliable source of protection and are used by everyone, including politicians. They do not address terrorism, and they supplement, rather than replace, politically approved local policing initiatives. The prevalence of militia groups may undermine international efforts to develop the FGS's capacity and legitimacy, but it does not undermine the government's efforts to provide legitimate governance and security because it has not to date provided any.

Terrorism and Counterterrorism

In the same way as Mogadishu's security environment is shaped by extremism, crime and under-development, and its problems are exacerbated by legacy issues and cultural and social preferences, its preferred forms of security governance and provision accommodate a variety of approaches. But the critical issue affecting decision-making and practice today – and the one acting as a concrete conceptualisation of the city's underlying insecurity – is terrorism and the need to develop an effective counterterrorism capability. This is not to suggest that the current level of insecurity is best seen as a struggle for control between the government and Al-Shabaab, the largest and most successful militant organisation operating in Somalia.[37] Rather, the consequences of terrorism potentially affect everyone, from politicians operating in Villa Somalia to children working in the fish market. There are many instances of Al-Shabaab targeting members of parliament, judges, elders and NGO activists, as well as representatives of the state such as tax collectors, police, soldiers and NISA agents.[38] There is also anecdotal evidence of Al-Shabaab gunmen being hired by residents to kill their business or political competitors.

The threat to all from terrorism is real and unpredictable. In addition to targeted assassinations, every month between October 2016 and October 2017 saw attacks involving vehicle-borne bombs, suicide bombers, improvised explosive devices (IEDs) and grenades, culminating in a lorry bomb that killed more than 300 people on 16 October 2017. Significantly, the devastation achieved by this bomb was caused by the lorry's load of several hundred kilograms of military-grade and homemade explosives

---

[37] For a concise overview of Al-Shabaab, see National Counterterrorism Center, 'Terrorist Groups', <https://www.dni.gov/nctc/groups.html>, accessed 4 December 2016. For details, see Stig Jarle Hansen, *Al-Shabaab in Somalia: The History and Ideology of a Militant Islamic Group* (London: Hurst, 2016). See also Jason Burke, 'Somalia Bombing May Have been Revenge for Botched US-led Operation', *The Guardian*, 17 October 2017.

[38] *Al-Jazeera*, 'Al-Shabab Attacks CID Headquarters in Mogadishu', 31 July 2016.

igniting as it stood beside a fuel tanker, resulting in a massive fireball.[39] All such incidents resulted in civilian casualties. As Michael Keating, Special Representative of the UN Secretary-General for Somalia, noted in April, 337 people were killed or injured by 87 IED incidents in the first three months of 2017, with civilian casualties from IEDs increasing by more than 50 per cent in the two years since 2015.[40]

Physical vulnerability is a particularly critical issue for police officers. The experience of Hussein Jiinow Afrah who, in his six years as an SPF policeman, was wounded on three separate occasions by IEDs, is not extreme: 'The shrapnel still lodged in my shoulder, groin and arm causes me no end of problems. But I feel lucky because many of my friends are dead. Al-Shabaab calls me from time to time to try and intimidate me and tell me to quit the force'.[41] Other examples involve Mogadishu's traffic police, which was relaunched as a sign of the city's vibrancy in 2011 and is regularly targeted by militia and government troops as well as Al-Shabaab.[42] The question then arises as to how police and residents understand, and respond to, terrorism.

Al-Shabaab is only one of the many problems confronting Mogadishu's inhabitants, and the organisation also offers practical solutions and benefits to some individuals and groups, include mediating local clan disputes, improving religious education, providing basic services, and institutionalising consultative bodies for local governance arrangements.[43] Nevertheless, anecdotal evidence suggests that terrorism and its associated dangers and vulnerabilities dominate many people's daily security calculations, and this situation is unlikely to change soon. Al-Shabaab, which advocates the Saudi-inspired Wahhabi version of Islam, lost control of Mogadishu in 2011, but retains the ability to operate in a way that is not fundamentally different to that of 2013 when the International Crisis Group (ICG) concluded that it is both an armed insurgent group and, more significantly, a movement representing a much deeper social phenomenon:

---

[39] See *Reuters*, 'Deadly Somalia Blast Reveals Flaws in Intelligence Efforts', 20 October 2017.

[40] Reliefweb, 'SRSG Keating Condemns Increased Attacks against Civilians', 11 April 2017, <https://reliefweb.int/report/somalia/srsg-keating-condemns-increased-attacks-against-civilians>, accessed 26 January 2018.

[41] Somalia Report, 'Somalia Portraits: Hussein Jiinow Afrah, Policeman', 28 April 2012, <piracyreport.com/index.php/post/3284>, accessed 26 January 2018.

[42] *Hiiraan Online*, 'Mogadishu's Traffic Cops Say They are Targeted by Militia, Gov't Troops', 30 January 2017.

[43] International Crisis Group (ICG), 'Somalia: Al-Shabaab – It Will Be a Long War', Policy Briefing No. 99, 26 June 2014, p. 2, <https://d2071andvip0wj.cloudfront.net/somalia-Al-Shabaab-it-will-be-a-long-war.pdf>, accessed 5 July 2014.

Even as it takes conventional losses, especially of territory, it apparently continues to infiltrate all walks and stations of Somali life, including some [FGS] agencies. A small but significant example is that at the end of 2013, it in effect controlled Mogadishu's Central Prison. The presence of Al-Shabaab suspects (just under half the prison's population) had changed the institution's character; the group's usual local structures of an emir, *hasba* (moral police), *Amniyat* (internal intelligence agency) and Shura, were all operating, and members were being paid.[44]

ICG considers that Al-Shabaab is likely to continue to thrive because of three factors, all of which are immune to military action: an ability to exploit clan sentiments; a fiscal strength and willingness to pay its soldiers and operatives well and regularly; and access to the regular revenue provided by the religious duty to give alms and charity.[45]

The Critical Role of Insecurity

Most scholarly and policy-relevant research focuses on security, rather than insecurity,[46] yet the central issue here is how best to develop security in the sense of making people feel less vulnerable, with such feelings exacerbated by terrorist attacks.

All sectors of society are exposed to a range of physical threats arising from inter-clan conflicts, Al-Shabaab attacks, revenge killings, trigger-happy guards, or conflict arising from land, property and live stock disputes, even if it is IDPs, the members of minority clans and women who experience this to an extreme degree. Women in IDP camps lack access to lockable shelters and safe lavatories and are particularly vulnerable to sexual violence, assault and rape, but most women are subject to physical assaults ranging from female genital mutilation and forced early marriage to domestic violence. The overall picture of danger, vulnerability and uncertainty is further reinforced by ambiguous contextual variables such as the suspicion and alienation felt by many, even if the relationship between the various elements is unclear. Thus, Somali youths (young men between the ages of approximately 15 and 35) face challenges which can make them vulnerable to recruitment by Al-Shabaab. As diaspora researcher Adam Yusuf Egal was told repeatedly, Somali culture excludes youth from

---

[44] *Ibid.*, pp. 12–17, emphasis in original. The Shura is a ten-man council.

[45] See DefenceWeb, 'al-Shabaab Inc', 25 May 2017, <http://www.defenceweb.co.za/index.php?option=com_content&view=article&id=47967>, accessed 26 January 2018.

[46] Insecurity is addressed by anthropology and development studies, rather than conflict studies, and is analysed primarily in terms of individual and societal responses to it. See, for example, Theodore Trefon (ed.), *Reinventing Order in the Congo: How People Respond to State Failure in Kinshasa* (London: Zed Books, 2005).

political participation because they are not considered mature or experienced enough to participate in formal meetings;[47] one respondent told him that young men have been deliberately marginalised by their elders and abandoned by their clans, the government and society at large. There are a small number of women district commissioners, but women and girls are generally unrepresented in the city's broader political and economic decision-making processes. However, this does not appear to act as an alienating factor in the way that it does for young men, although it is not known as yet how this affects their contact with police or attitudes to the government. Overall, international analysts and advisers know remarkably little about Somali perspectives on insecurity, and what is known is gleaned from a combination of work such as OCVP surveys addressing people's perceptions of security,[48] unpublished reports by Somali NGOs, and the work of researchers such as Egal.[49] As a first step towards rebalancing the picture, it is necessary to consider how the security environment is currently assessed by Somalis and, equally importantly, to engage with the issue at the heart of Mogadishu's predicament: how to make the city safer or, more accurately, how to lessen insecurity.

Mitigating Mogadishu's Vulnerabilities
When Egal asked ten police officers and ten residents who had lived in the city for more than ten years and were educated to at least secondary school level what they understood by terrorism, all emphasised its destructive and political nature.[50] For example, a 25-year-old male graduate working for an NGO and a woman postgraduate lecturer stressed the difficulty of defining terrorism, with both emphasising its destructive intent; the man stressed that terrorism means 'killing innocent people for the sake of politics, economics and religion' while the woman argued that 'it involves using violence to reach certain goals and the aim is to frighten the society'. A 38-year-old police inspector said terrorism involves 'threatening people and killing their lives and the life of their families through shooting, suicide bomb and beheading them', while a senior police officer defined it as 'killing, hurting, and threatening people because of their different point of view, their religion, and their racial ethnic origin and the aim is to reach political

---

[47] Egal, 'Police Corruption, Radicalization and Terrorist Attacks in Mogadishu', pp. 45–57; see, UNDP, 'Somalia Human Development Report 2012', p. 18.
[48] For an overview of OCVP's Mogadishu surveys, see Heritage Institute of Policy Studies, 'Perceptions of Security and Justice in Mogadishu'.
[49] Menkhaus, 'Non-State Security Providers and Political Formation in Somalia'.
[50] Egal, 'Police Corruption, Radicalization and Terrorist Attacks in Mogadishu', pp. 27–30.

agenda'. A 35-year-old woman nurse was equally clear: 'terrorism is nothing but killing threatening people to achieve political goals'. She added that Al-Shabaab may claim to fight on behalf of the message that Mohammad is the messenger of God, but 'the truth is that they have political agenda in their mind'.

Egal's respondents were equally clear about the meaning of radicalisation, which they defined as 'brainwashing young people to become terrorists' (a 45-year-old businessman) or 'becoming isolated from mainstream public and adopting extreme radical views that turns you to see your people as your enemy' (a 35-year-old civil society worker). Two security officers had clearly given the topic previous thought. Thus a 45-year-old junior-rank police officer argued that people are radicalised in one of two ways: 'one is called self-radicalisation and someone else radicalises the other one. Self-radicalisation is like one understanding and interpreting the religion and the world in a wrong way and adopting radical views that turns him to act in a violent way. The other one is brainwashing'. A NISA bomb disposal expert was equally emphatic that radicalisation is 'a complex process that individuals go through from becoming extreme from mainstream, isolating from family friends and society at large and searching identity and belonging. It is not necessarily that radicalized people to become terrorist [sic] but each terrorist has gone through the process of radicalization'.[51]

Egal's respondents emphasise the immediate and destructive power of terrorism. Although their response to donor claims that meaningful security depends on the FGS and Benadir's administration addressing such long-term issues as under-development and factional political culture is not known,[52] it is clear that Mogadishu's security provision is driven by the need to immediately respond to the threat posed by Al-Shabaab. However, sequencing the response is complicated by Al-Shabaab's skill at exploiting underlying societal norms and tensions. As Ilya Gridneff noted in the aftermath of the bomb attack in January 2017 on the Dayah Hotel, Al-Shabaab's influence owes more to its strategy of capitalising on clan

---

[51] *Ibid.*, p. 29. As Egal notes, Somali experience is comparable to that elsewhere in the world. It confirms the assessment of, for example, Peter Neumann, 'The Trouble with Radicalization', *International Affairs* (Vol. 89, No. 4, 2013) and Fernando Reinares et al., 'Radicalisation Processes Leading to Acts of Terrorism: A Concise Report Prepared by the European Commission's Expert Group on Violent Radicalisation', 15 May 2008, <http://www.rikcoolsaet.be/files/art_ip_wz/Expert%20Group%20Report%20Violent%20Radicalisation%20FINAL.pdf.>, accessed 4 February 2017.

[52] See M J Fox, *The Roots of Somali Political Culture* (Boulder, CO: Lynne Rienner, 2015).

and political grievances than to the appeal of its jihadist ideology.[53] The hotel bombing can be regarded as an attack on Somalia's exclusionary political process; many elders and recently elected MPs from the Rahanweyn clan or, more specifically, its Digil-Mirifle sub-clans used the hotel to conduct election-related meetings with dealmakers and high-profile officials, while youths were systematically excluded. Gridneff adds that such attacks emphasise that Al-Shabaab will not be defeated on the battlefield but through political engagement that prevents it from exploiting gaps in Somalia's security architecture. This is understandable, but will nevertheless take more time than is available to the federal authorities. As newly elected President Farmajo noted on 8 February 2017, the key tasks confronting him include not only addressing security, but also dealing with corruption, ineffective governance, drought and, critically, paying the Somali soldiers responsible for fighting Al-Shabaab, with which Somalia 'is in a state of war'.[54] In practice, as ICG has repeatedly noted,[55] addressing these issues requires the same mix of pragmatism and political skill that Al-Shabaab displays.

One other issue deserves note. The security challenges confronting Farmajo reflect Somalia's short-term political culture and a lack of technical discipline that increases the authorities' uncoordinated short-term responses. But even if Farmajo is willing or able to address the challenges, much will depend on the attitude and response of the 2.5 million inhabitants spread across the city's seventeen districts. In a city such as Mogadishu, everything depends on the willingness of residents to report strangers or suspicious incidents to the police or district authorities – but it is often dangerous to be seen with the unresponsive and distrusted police, while some district commissioners ignore the government and prevent the police from operating in their district, preferring to run their own protection and extortion rackets.[56] Meanwhile, the international community has little knowledge of the details of police–community relations, and scholarly research focuses on the militia and clan groups providing the bulk of the city's security provision, or on informal community policing in specific locations to the exclusion of its interaction with the formal sector.[57]

---

[53] Ilya Gridneff, 'Al-Shabaab Strategy Shifts Toward Clans as Presidential Election Loom', IPI Global Observatory, 27 January 2017.

[54] BBC Somali Analyses, 'Five Big Challenges Newly Elected President Farmajo Should Address Immediately', 9 February 2017, <http://somaliamediamonitoring. org/february-9-2017-daily-monitoring-report/>, accessed 14 February 2017.

[55] ICG, 'Somalia', p. 20.

[56] Menkhaus, 'Non-State Security Providers and Political Formation in Somalia', p. 24.

[57] Ibid.; Mohamed Ahmed Jama, 'Community Policing in Mogadishu: A Case Study of Bakhara Market', Humanitarian Practice Network, October 2008, <http://odihpn.

Government Responses

Two practical responses to the security issue are significant: the Mogadishu city security plan and the Waberi district neighbourhood-watch scheme, both of which are driven by fears about Al-Shabaab's activities. Both help to fill gaps in the understanding of the situation on the ground because both address the time-urgent needs of counterterrorism, as well as the community mobilisation and cohesion it ideally requires. Equally, both stress Somalis' comprehensive understanding of security while emphasising the ease with which security for counterterrorism purposes merges into security for development-oriented goals. What is more, the two complement each other; Mogadishu's city security plan requires substantial resources, whereas the neighbourhood-watch scheme shows what can be achieved with minimal resources. In other words, making Mogadishu safer requires not only institution- and capacity-building, but also a minimal and locally acceptable working relationship between residents and government authorities, such as the SPF and NISA. Ironically, Al-Shabaab's activities may be said to have encouraged not only a city-wide counterterrorism plan; but also a notable degree of community cohesion and mobilisation.

The FGS's risk assessment of these issues is unclear, although NISA's robust methods for gaining intelligence offer a good indication of the FGS's preferred approach; NISA agents routinely carry out mass sweeps, despite having no legal mandate to arrest or detain suspects, and they hold and mistreat detainees for long periods without following due process.[58] In practice, sweeps are a common tactic for both NISA and the police, gun fights are frequent, and 'police members' who arrest or kill Al-Shabaab 'assassins' receive 'monetary awards'.[59] Thus, in the course of a house-to-house search

---

org/magazine/community-policing-in-mogadishu-a-case-study-of-bakhara-market/ >, accessed 14 January 2018. Since approximately 2010, academics' preferred approach to police and policing provision has focused on the informal or community-based groups providing the bulk of Africa's everyday security and justice. See, for example, Helene Mariae Kyed, 'Introduction to the Special Issue Legal Pluralism and International Development Interventions', *Journal of Legal Pluralism and Unofficial Law* (Vol. 43, No. 63, 2013), pp. 1–23.

[58] US State Department, 'Somalia 2015 Human Rights Report', 2016, p. 4, <https:// www.state.gov/documents/organization/252939.pdf>, accessed 12 December 2016; *Waagacusub*, 'Video: NISA Tortures a Government Worker', 22 May 2016, <http://waagacusub.net/articles/2027/Somalia-Video-NISA-tortures-a-government-worker>, accessed 5 July 2016.

[59] In 2016, Dhacdo.com reported that '[S]ecurity branches continue to promise monetary awards for police members who either arrest or kill Al-Shabaab assassins'. See *AMISOM Media Monitoring*, '20 Arrested in Mogadishu Security Operation', 3 October 2016, <http://somaliamediamonitoring.org/november-3-2016-daily-monitoring-report/>, accessed 4 October 2016.

in a neighbourhood of Wadajir district on 28 September 2016, heavily armed 'security forces' arrested 20 young men suspected of being members of Al-Shabaab. Several days later, an Al-Shabaab assassin who had killed a senior security official in Hodan district was shot dead while two suspected assassins were injured in a gun fight. Such operations intensified in the run-up to the presidential elections, when SNA and AMISOM forces arrested dozens of youths in Wadajir and Waberi in a bid to prevent Al-Shabaab attacks.[60]

The response of the FGS is influenced theoretically by the advice and resources it receives from donors such as the US and UK, for whom improving security and security-relevant skills is a priority. On this, General Thomas Waldhauser, Commander of AFRICOM, is explicit: 'What's needed in Somalia is a co-ordinated punch – search and destroy Al-Shabaab'.[61] However, in practice, the ability of donors to influence the Somali authorities is severely restricted, as is their capacity to shape the relationship between the FGS, Benadir's administration (and, in particular, the mayor's office) and Mogadishu's inhabitants. This is especially evident in the case of the UK. On the other hand, while the US's coercive power, technical prestige and resources ensure that it has influence over Somali security actors, the muted Somali response to the UK's limited agenda is as informative. Importantly, the UK's involvement in implementing the city's security plan and neighbourhood-watch scheme over a period of several years increases understanding of the relationship between two critical aspects of contemporary security: counterterrorism as an exemplar of state-focused security and community safety as an expression of what the OECD calls 'people-centred security'.[62] Admittedly, approaching this from a UK perspective offers an unbalanced picture of Somali responses. Nevertheless, donor resources probably affect many Somali calculations, albeit negatively, temporarily or superficially, and exploring the city's security plan and neighbourhood-watch scheme in this way helps to fill some of the gaps about how Somalis in both the administration and the districts understand their security environment and seek to manage threats.

International Policy Perspectives

The UK prioritises counterterrorism. It also prioritises Mogadishu; it is the second-largest donor to Somalia after the US, and its embassy, which

---

[60] *Shabelle News*, 'SNA, AMISOM Forces Carry Out Sweep in Mogadishu', 4 February 2017.

[61] Chege Mbitiru, 'Special Forces May Soon Join the War Against Al-Shabaab', *Daily Nation*, 5 March 2017.

[62] OECD DAC, *Handbook on Security System Reform: Supporting Security and Justice* (Paris: OECD, 2007), pp. 14, 89.

opened in 2013, was for several years the only EU embassy in the city.[63] This may reflect its historical interest in Somalia or the threat associated with the continuing activities of Al-Shabaab, or, more probably, the presence of a large Somali diaspora in the UK and the fear of UK citizens travelling to training camps in the Horn of Africa and returning to conduct terrorist attacks in the UK. Consequently, the UK, like the US and Turkey, actively seeks to improve the performance of Somalia's anti-terrorism units.[64]

At the same time, the UK's political approach is explicitly shaped by the notion of a security–development nexus whereby there can be no security without development and no development without security,[65] and is arguably driven by its commitment to spend 0.7 per cent of the UK's gross national income on aid every year.[66] According to the UK's National Security Council, 'there is no distinction between reducing poverty, tackling global challenges and serving our national interest – all are inextricably linked'.[67] Consequently, the UK places 'increased access to services for the most vulnerable to help support a wider process of peace and stability' alongside high-level objectives

[63] OECD DAC, 'Aid at a Glance Charts: Somalia'.
[64] *Intelligence Online*, 'Training Somalia's Anti-Terrorism Units', No. 777, 22 February 2017. Turkey has been Somalia's main benefactor and overseas partner since August 2011 when then-Prime Minister Recep Tayyip Erdogan became the first non-African leader to visit the country in two decades. Domestic concerns ensure that Turkey supports counterterrorism operations in Somalia and Kenya; its agenda focuses on the Fetullah Terrorist Organisation (FETO), which Erdogan blames for the attempted coup in July 2016. See also *Daily Sabah*, 'Turkey Opens Biggest Overseas Military Base in Somalia', 30 September 2017; Mahad Wasuge, 'Turkey's Assistance Model in Somalia: Achieving Much with Little', Heritage Institute for Policy Studies, 2016, <http://www.heritageinstitute.org/wp-content/uploads/2016/02/Turkeys-Assistance-Model-in-Somalia-Achieving-Much-With-Little1-1.pdf>, accessed 7 March 2017.
[65] For the original debate, see Mark Duffield, *Global Governance and the New Wars: The Merging of Development and Security* (London: Zed Books, 2001); see also Lars Buur, Steffan Jensen and Finn Stepputat (eds), *The Security–Development Nexus: Expressions of Sovereignty and Securitization in Southern Africa* (Cape Town: Nordiska Afrikainstitutet, 2007). For the perspectives that result, see Joanna Spear and Paul Williams (eds), *Security and Development in Global Politics: A Critical Comparison* (Washington, DC: Georgetown University Press, 2012).
[66] Sophie Jamieson, 'Priti Patel Sets Out New Vision to Stop International Aid Budget Being "Stolen" and "Wasted"', *Daily Telegraph*, 14 September 2016.
[67] HM Treasury and Department for International Development (DFID), *UK Aid: Tackling Global Challenges in the National Interest*, Cm 9163 (London: The Stationery Office, 2015), p. 4.

targeting state formation and peacebuilding.[68] However, while the UK's security interests are undoubtedly prioritised, little of the £445 million (92 per cent) that DFID took from the UK's £484 million Somalia budget for 2009–14 was allocated to everyday street-level security.[69] Indeed, many of its police and defence-related activities are little more than tokenism.[70] This leaves the security element in the UK's Somalia policy opaque, covering everything from intelligence training for newly appointed diaspora officials to building a new regional police headquarters, to buying beds for a rehabilitation centre for former Al-Shabaab members.[71]

In practice, the UK's approach to security governance does not offer a realistic solution for a city such as Mogadishu because it downplays Somalia's underlying political economy, clan-based power dynamics, and the internecine rivalries associated with the allocation of desirable security resources. Somali officers may value the experience and technical resources of the UK's special operations professionals, but the UK's broadly liberal approach to security governance lacks traction when the entrepreneurs driving Somali politics and security operations pursue a style of governance that offers little to the city's malnourished, illiterate or unemployed inhabitants.[72] President Farmajo and some of the educated and relatively rich former diaspora Somalis now fulfilling governance roles may be more supportive of international goals than their predecessors, but little is likely to change in the short to medium term. Nevertheless, these considerations do not detract from the fact that in Mogadishu effective counterterrorism depends on the willingness of residents to monitor and report suspicious incidents to the authorities. This in turn requires a degree of community safety and cohesion. The ways in which the various elements relate are evident in the city's security plans, the capstone of which is the Mogadishu city security plan.

Mogadishu's City Security Plan

It was not until 2015 that Benadir's regional administration acknowledged the threat posed by Al-Shabaab – and the FGS's inability to gather the community intelligence to manage it – by developing and implementing a

---

[68] See DFID, 'Business Case: NGO Health Consortium Somalia (HCS) Extension', p. 4, <http://iati.dfid.gov.uk/iati_documents/3717709.odt>, accessed 9 December 2016.
[69] Author's private conversation with UK analyst, London, August 2016.
[70] Hills, 'Making Mogadishu Safe', p. 11.
[71] Author conversations with UK consultants, Mogadishu and London, July 2016 and October 2016.
[72] De Waal, *The Real Politics of the Horn of Africa*, pp. 109–29.

Mogadishu city security plan.[73] The original initiative appears to have been Somali-driven, but its organisational development was soon shaped by the UK, which has actively encouraged the regional administration to adopt an integrated and multi-agency approach to security, albeit with an emphasis on counterterrorism. This is evident in the plan's slogan of 'a network to defeat a network'.

The need to anticipate, address and prevent terrorist attacks dominates the calculations of both Somalia and the UK. In theory, the specialist skills found in the plan's units – including the Joint Intelligence Management Cell (JIMC), Tactical Operations Center (TOC), and Joint Operations Coordination Center (JOCC)[74] – should make the regional administration's response more efficient and effective. It should also play to the UK's technical and political strengths, enabling it to influence the government and the regional administration and promote its own concerns while helping Somalis to develop the legitimate and functional government the international community advocates. Indeed, the relevance of the plan is clear from the multiple instances of suicide bombers or fighters ramming cars into Aden Adde International Airport's AMISOM-guarded entry points to delay the presidential election; thirteen people died in an attack on 26 July 2016 and three on 2 January 2017.[75] But in fact, the results of UK policies are uneven; the UK's culturally specific terminology and procedures are applied to Somali practices, while flagship technical projects such as the MCSP's Joint Operating Coordination Centre (JOCC) are prioritised over sustainable but low-level activities in the districts. Even so, the record of Mogadishu's city security plan offers insights into the details of intelligence collection in a chronically insecure and bureaucratically dysfunctional city. Additionally, it illustrates the ways in which Somalis adapt international procedures and technologies to suit local conditions.

The JOCC, which is mandated by the Somali National Security Policy and the Minister of Internal Security's strategy, and is supported by the Ministries of Internal Security, Defence and Justice, as well as the Benadir administration and AMISOM's force commander, is organised and presented in terms that reflect the UK's experience, expectations and interests. It has a dedicated suite of facilities equipped with computers and is described as having 'primacy' for multi-agency intelligence collection

---

[73] Hills, 'Making Mogadishu Safe'.
[74] These acronyms, which reflect the influence of UK and US technical advisers, are in daily use in the offices supporting the city's security plan.
[75] *Reuters*, '13 People Killed in Somali Suicide Bombing Claimed by al Shabaab', 26 July 2016; *Reuters*, 'Suicide Bombers Attack Peacekeepers' Somali HQ, At Least Three Dead', 2 January 2017.

and crisis response, with the latter provided by a standing 'Gold' command centre for Mogadishu, to which the regional heads of the security agencies contribute. In order to fulfil its role in intelligence development, the JOCC depends on verifiable good-quality intelligence from flows provided by a number of Somali and international organisations. These include NISA, the police, the national army, the Immigration and Naturalization Directorate, the Somali Correction Corps, AMISOM, specialist organisations from the international community, a well-connected NGO called Somali Women Against Violent Extremism (SWAVE), and neighbourhood-watch schemes. Although neighbourhood-watch schemes operate at the entry level in terms of intelligence flows, their importance here lies in their position as a conduit for information from the district security committees through the district information management centres that play a key part in the city security plan. The district security committees implement the national and city security plans at district level and help to determine the operational priorities of the SPF and NISA.

The JIMC collates the information received and develops a common operating picture that allows it to develop the actionable intelligence needed for targeting Al-Shabaab's networks. This arrangement acknowledges the role of community information and mobilisation in developing intelligence, although the UK and the US also promote technical solutions, such as a Geographical Information System designed to collate the multi-agency information required to efficiently produce a common operating picture. For now, the regular presence of international advisers ensures that the system works relatively smoothly; Somali officials and officers attend multi-agency targeting and planning meetings and ICT-based work is completed, despite intermittent internet connectivity. Whether such a model is sustainable is, however, debateable, given its dependence on international support.

In reality, the overall picture of Mogadishu's formal security management is more nuanced than the city security plan's record might suggest because terrorism is only one aspect of the fluid and overlapping security environment, albeit the one with the highest profile. For everyday security purposes, people look to informal providers to keep themselves and their property safe, although surveys show that many residents would consider reporting crime to the police, provided that a locally acceptable form of community-oriented policing could be developed. For such reasons, discussions of security in Mogadishu need to address issues ranging from high-level counterterrorism down to street-level reporting, with police–community relations a connecting link. The relationship between these issues is significant because, as Mogadishu's Heritage Institute for Policy Studies notes, the security threats facing Mogadishu 'appear to be mutually reinforcing and interconnected', with most residents agreeing that 'there is a relationship between socio-economic conditions and levels of crime'.[76] Identifying the points at which the various aspects interact – and where they shift categories – is important for both analytical and empirical reasons. It offers potential insights into not only the police–community engagement which, donors assume, drives or reflects effective policing at the local level, but also into the nature of change and political and institutional tipping points. But the process is far from straightforward, and analysis is made difficult by the complex nature of the Somali polity and its notions of the police role. How, then, do Mogadishu's officers and inhabitants understand the police role and how do they interact with police officers?

Somali-Style Policing

Mogadishu's insecurity, the SPF's minimal policing role, and academics' focus on non-state actors ensures that little is known about Somali police culture or everyday police business; donors and many international technical advisers are more concerned to reform or improve the SPF's technical standards and practices than to understand it on its own terms. In fact, little is known about how it recruits, whose agenda it prioritises, and how officers spend their day.[77] International trainers working with elite reaction units say that the *esprit de corps* found in such units has weakened the hold of clan affiliation, while advisers working with general duties officers say that the SPF is less clan-dominated than it was, or, more accurately, that the groups involved are now more representative, even if mobile units such as the Darwish remain clan-oriented – but much remains unclear.[78] AMISOM and the UNDP have for some years conducted vetting and training projects, but there are no open-source assessments of the results and AMISOM's reports offer little more than a public relations exercise for its online police magazine. The clan affiliation and curriculum vitae of senior officers are widely known among Mogadishu's inhabitants, but internationals rarely know more than a few background details about a handful of high-profile individuals.[79] Lieutenant Colonel Zakia Hussein is a case in point. Former diaspora and

---

[76] Heritage Institute for Policy Studies (HIPS), 'Perceptions of Security and Justice in Mogadishu: Interpreting Results of the OCVP Conflict and Security Assessment', Policy Brief No. 8, September 2014, p. 2, <http://www.heritageinstitute.org/wp-content/uploads/2014/09/HIPS_Policy_Brief_008_2014_ENGLISH.pdf>, accessed 4 March 2015.

[77] See Alice Hills, 'What is Policeness? On Being Police in Somalia', *British Journal of Criminology* (Vol. 54, No. 5, 2014), pp. 765–83.

[78] Author personal communication with UK trainer, Mogadishu, 22 July 2016.

without police experience, she was appointed initially as the SPF's director of community policing and has since become the head of CID.[80]

Nevertheless, two key observations deserve note, not least because researchers are rediscovering the usefulness of police for Africa's populace. First, the SPF presents an outwardly conventional and politically legitimate appearance, celebrating its 74th anniversary on 20 December 2017; its claim to be the direct and legitimate successor of the widely respected force founded in 1943 is seemingly accepted by the police forces of Somaliland and Puntland. It is structured on lines common throughout Africa and its educated officers are familiar with international practices and procedures, even if they filter them through local interests and dispositions.[81] Like their peers elsewhere, Somali officers respond to imported practices in an adaptive manner, integrating useful or valuable aspects of international understanding into local realities and personal or group experience. Many are also experienced and successful fighters or, in the term locally used, 'soldier-policemen'. After all, the distinction between a policeman, a militiaman and a soldier is not always clear when they all fight and wear similar items of clothing. The overview of Somali police forces provided by the *SomaliaReport* news network in 2012 remains relevant. Levels of violence have since lessened, but Al-Shabaab's presence means that policing remains a rudimentary and dangerous business. SPF officers are rarely seen in the streets, and the poor quality of their weaponry is a source of grievance. More importantly, the SPF's role continues to be affected by tensions between the legal pluralism of the customary, traditional and Islamic law underpinning Somali expectations, and donors' desire to integrate it into Western policing structures.[82]

Second, as this implies, the SPF's reality is different from that promoted by international organisations and donors because it reflects the difference between security delivered by the state (as in the UK) and security delivered through social processes in a legally plural society. It reflects local practices and priorities as well, many of which concern money or property. Indeed, the lure of stipends is often the only meaningful tool donors can use to connect with local police; officers are

---

[79] Ex-diaspora cultural advisers working for international organisations speak of having been to school with, for example, senior officers in NISA and the Immigration Department.
[80] Dalsan Radio, 'Somalia: Lt. Colonel Zakia Hussein! Against All Odds', *All Africa*, 28 June 2014.
[81] For further details about the SPF's formal organisation, see Somaligov, 'Welcome to the Somali Police', <http://www.police.somaligov.net/Chief%20of%20Somali%20CID.html>, accessed 10 April 2017.
[82] Young Pelton, Nuxurkey and Osman, 'The Police of Somalia, Somaliland, Puntland'.

paid $100 regardless of rank – but only if they go to work, and this must affect everyday police business. The attitude of an officer in a specialist reaction unit in July 2016 is informative; after an absence of six years (which is not unusual) he had planned to visit his family, but changed his mind when it was pointed out that he would not get paid for the two months he intended to spend with them.

However, none of this means that Somali officers are not police or that 'a police force in the Western sense is … an alien institution'.[83] Regardless of their appearance or ability to provide order or security, police officers exhibit a quality that is perceived by both Somalis and international organisations, such as the UNDP and the African Union (AU), as 'policeness' and as linking the state (or, in this case, the FGS) and society in some way. And this is understandable because they share occupational commonalities and a technical vocabulary with police in other regions, and are in some cases consciously developing the complexity of practices, procedures and norms required for the capacity-building through which the state is thought to emerge and be expressed.

Contextual Factors

The commonalities the SPF shares with police in other regions are offset by Somali social processes and cultural continuities, such as clannism and customary law. These are more influential than either international policing models or state-based authority, and notions of what it means to be police – and, consequently, what police–community engagement might look like – must accommodate this. The overall picture is complicated by three additional factors.

First, while it is generally agreed that a monopoly on the politically legitimate use of coercion is a defining element of the police role,[84] socially sanctioned physical coercion already plays a significant role in daily life in Mogadishu, and the Somali preference for negotiation, informal arrangements and tactical manoeuvre is usually underpinned by the threat of physical or political violence.[85] Further, the technical skills associated with the specialist coercive knowledge that is policing are valued as a means to a practical end. Rather than being a service, policing is seen as a commodity, a business opportunity and an expression of

---

[83] Martin Murphy, *Somalia: The New Barbary? Piracy and Islam in the Horn of Africa* (London: Hurst, 2011), p. 156. For further insight into Western policing, see Peter Manning, *Democratic Policing in a Changing World* (Boulder, CO: Paradigm, 2011).

[84] Egon Bittner, *The Functions of the Police in Modern Society* (Washington, DC: National Institute of Mental Health, 1970).

[85] Markus Höehne and Virginia Luling (eds), *Milk and Peace, Drought and War: Somali Culture, Society and Politics* (London: Hurst, 2010).

power relations; it is part of the same political dynamics as clannism, conflict, entrepreneurialism and fragmentation, not least because Mogadishu is the site of multiple conflicts over territory, trade monopolies and political power fought by people with no interest in institutions or security forces they cannot control.[86] Additionally, the danger of being assassinated must isolate police officers or, more probably, enhance their attachment to the clan-based commitments and obligations that are the only guarantees they have to deal with the consequences of physical danger, inadequate equipment and irregular pay.

At the same time, the second factor is the continuing influence of memories of the effective but repressive policing enforced by former President Barre (who fled Mogadishu in 1991, but had been in power since 1969); senior officers and officials with experience of policing during the Barre era acknowledge the technical attractions of its institutional structures even as they emphasise that its brutality must be avoided. The attraction of Barre-style security is even stronger for Somalia's intelligence agencies, which are of higher status than its police; the US's CIA supports NISA, just as it supports the intelligence agencies in Somaliland and Puntland, and many powerful clans have created agencies modelled on Barre's intelligence agency, which was by far that era's strongest institution.[87] Consequently, while individual Somalis have different experiences of life during the 1980s and 1990s, and differing visions of Somalia's future, there is a consensus on what police should look like that is reinforced by many senior officers having a history of international contact.

The third factor that complicates the picture – legal pluralism – is especially important in this context. This is particularly true for influential senior officers who are aware of international policing practices but must navigate between the contradictory demands of the FGS's need for counterterrorism operations, mayoral politics, local or clan-based calculations and imperatives, and donors' insistence on democratic policing, with all of them displaying flexibility. Additionally, Somalis look first to customary law and local or traditional non-state actors, such as elders or Sharia Law, rather than to the police, and officers engage with local elders and district security committees about daily issues such as land or water rights and goat theft only when invited. Indeed, legal pluralism is probably the major challenge to Western conceptions of what it means to be a police officer in Somalia.

---

[86] Hills, 'Somalia Works'.
[87] Liban Ahmad, 'Somalia's Intelligence Services Mimicry', *Pan African Newswire*, 1 February 2013.

Linked to this is the need for police officers to consult with a range of alternative policing providers, for policing is provided by militia and clan groups loyal to factional leaders and district commissioners as well as businessmen and Sharia courts. Unsurprisingly, combinations of formal and informal providers are common, as an example from July 2011 shows: security in Dharkenley district improved significantly as a result of the combined efforts of an experienced cross-clan militia made up of officers who had served under Barre (the Hillac brigade), youth militias (*madani*), a Sufi militia (Ahlu-Sunna Wal-Jama, which was theoretically aligned to the FGS but actually operated autonomously) and the district's police.[88] Admittedly, international-style policing also displays a degree of flexibility, discretion and pragmatism, but it offsets this with a hierarchical and bureaucratic organisation that is missing in Somalia. Consequently, it could be that Mogadishu's policing – and police–community relations – are best understood as projects of changing social and political processes within unequal fields of power (albeit conventionally organised), with the emphasis on accommodation and flexibility.[89]

In this way, local norms and practices, legacy issues and personal experience provide Mogadishu's police officers with a layered knowledge base of what to do and, critically, how to survive and how to treat the residents. It ensures that they have a range of resources for coping with the consequences of insecurity with the most successful blending of personal experience, local ties, contextual knowledge and informal responses.[90] Their role is also affected by factors such as Somalis prioritising reconciliation and reparation over retribution and punishment, and preferring informal alternatives to formal sentencing and detention facilities – although this amounts to little in Mogadishu because the functional judicial system required to make this meaningful does not exist. Customary law is more powerful than formal institutions and elders are used to solve, manage and negotiate issues; government (secular) law, and its associated institutions, is the weakest of all. Even so, cooperative arrangements exist, with militias loyal to Mogadishu's district commissioners ensuring that people returning to their neighbourhoods after having been away register at a police station. Meanwhile, the police accommodate civil society initiatives by providing surveillance and reporting: 'they tell us'.

---

[88] Police Advisory Committee (PAC), 'Report on the Somali Police Force, July 2011', Mogadishu, 2011.

[89] Peter Little, *Somalia: Economy Without State* (Oxford: James Currey, 2003), p. 3.

[90] This also applies to politicians; see, for example, Marleen Renders, *Consider Somaliland: State-Building with Traditional Leaders and Institutions* (Leiden: Brill, 2012).

Conclusions

Mogadishu's environment is shaped by insecurity and power-related rivalries, with terrorism and physical violence potentially affecting the lives of everyone. The responses used by the city's authorities range from the raids, sweeps, curfews and intelligence-gathering associated with conventional counterterrorism operations involving NISA's agents to softer forms of community safety reliant on informal clan-based groups or the neighbourhood-watch schemes discussed in Chapter III. Influential international actors, the FGS and Benadir's Regional Administration emphasise the need for counterterrorism, whereas residents in the city's crowded districts look for protection, of people and property, with provision determined according to clan-based identity or networks. Donors see the resultant picture as unsatisfactory because it is opaque and operates independently of the state-based institutional responses at the heart of the international agenda for Somalia, whereas Somalis see a range of fluid, overlapping, coherent and locally acceptable responses to a series of interconnected and mutually reinforcing threats. Both see the Somali police as a visible sign of the FGS's aspirations to authority and legitimacy.

The role of the SPF in counterterrorism and community safety has yet to be analysed rigorously by the international advisers seeking to influence its development. Assuming that police–community relations offer an entrance into Mogadishu's security environment, and based on the dynamics found in police forces elsewhere in the region, the argument here is that the key to understanding meaningful police–community engagement is in the knowledge, skills and resources police need to fulfil societal, rather than international, expectations. This raises questions such as why, when and how people communicate with police, and whether different demographic or societal groups do so differently. Only by considering such issues can we understand the ways in which the Benadir administration, SPF and NISA collect the personal knowledge and community intelligence needed for successful security operations that will be capable of dislocating Al-Shabaab's networks and moderating the attractions of extremism in the face of Mogadishu's dysfunctional governance and volatility.

III. MANAGING NEIGHBOURHOOD SECURITY

Insecurity is Mogadishu's great leveller. On Saturday 26 November 2016, at least eleven people were killed and many more injured in a car bomb attack on a police checkpoint by a busy vegetable market in Waberi district.[1] No-one claimed responsibility, but most people thought that Al-Shabaab was behind the attack, which took place when the president was visiting a nearby university. Two weeks later, on Sunday 11 December 2016, a bomber drove a minibus packed with explosives into a tax office at the entrance to Mogadishu's Turkish-run seaport.[2] The blast went off among stalls in a lay-by crowded with day-shift workers buying breakfast. On this occasion Al-Shabaab claimed responsibility for killing 30 police officers, but most people agree that the majority of those killed and wounded were civilians and port employees. The blast could be heard across the city and pictures of the scene soon circulated on social media.[3]

The weeks between December's attack and February's presidential elections saw multiple assaults involving vehicle bombs, IEDs, grenades and targeted assassinations, which destroyed buildings and killed or injured government representatives and citizens. The elections were held in the safety of Aden Adde International Airport, but those without international protection were targeted by gunmen, including senior Somali security officers, government representatives such as tax collectors, and authority figures including elders, businessmen and NGO activists.[4]

---

[1] *Al Jazeera*, 'Car Bomb Attack Hits Somalia's Mogadishu', 26 November 2016.
[2] Harun Maruf, '20 Killed in Blast Near Mogadishu Port', *VOA*, 11 December 2016.
[3] *Al Jazeera*, 'Car Bomb Attack Hits Somalia's Mogadishu's Waberi District', 12 November 2016; *Shabelle News*, 'Al Shabaab Says Behind Deadly Attack in Mogadishu', 11 December 2016.
[4] *Al Jazeera*, 'Dozens Killed in Mogadishu Market Blast', 20 February 2017; *Garowe Online*, '4 Killed in Separate Shootings in Mogadishu and Afgoye', 6 January 2018, <https://www.garoweonline.com/index.php/en/news/somalia/somalia-4-killed-in-separate-shootings-in-mogadishu-and-afgoye>, accessed 10 January 2018.

None of this was new or unexpected. Furthermore, as the FGS's information minister Abdirahman Omar Osman told Horn Cable TV in June 2017, not all assassinations were the work of Al-Shabaab: 'We have come to a conclusion that armed assassinations and shootings in Mogadishu were not only planned and executed by Al-Shabaab',[5] but also by armed militia groups, such as that led by 'Mahad Dollar', who was arrested in Hodan on 30 May after an electoral delegate was killed. Curfews and road blocks were in place, especially in busy and notoriously dangerous areas such as KM4, Soobe and Benadir, where the drivers of small cars were targeted even as 'big trucks and public transport vehicles' were allowed to pass without being searched.[6] Security advisers may have feared for the airport buildings in which clan delegates voted, but policemen and tax-collectors working in the normally busy streets are always vulnerable, as are people passing by. Most of the women responding to surveys conducted by OCVP since 2014 say that bombings and explosions are their main concern, even in relatively safe districts, and suicide attacks and targeted killings are repeatedly cited as the most serious threats to personal and community safety.[7] In the circumstances, conventional distinctions between state and people-centred security mean little.[8]

The physical insecurity associated with terrorism and armed militiamen affects most of the city's inhabitants, but so does dealing with everyday contingencies such as injuries, accidents and fire. Indeed, fire is a common occurrence in markets such as Bakara, the largest in Somalia, and local people must deal with it on their own; Mogadishu reportedly has only five fire trucks, all donated by the City of London, and firefighters' pay is months in arrears.[9] Approximately half of Mogadishu's 2.5 million inhabitants are thought to live in poverty, which is acute even by regional standards,[10] while the lot of the city's IDPs is often desperate; in 2015, the population of the 160 IDP settlements in Daynile and Kahda

---

[5] *AMISOM Daily Monitoring Report*, 'Minister Defends Stabilization Operation, Cites Killings in the Capital', 5 June 2017.
[6] *AMISOM Media Monitoring*, 'Sweeping Security Operations in Progress in Mogadishu', 12 June 2017.
[7] OCVP, 'Central Zone – Conflict and Security Assessment Report: Central Zone', p. 12.
[8] See also OECD, 'Security System Reform and Governance', DAC Guidelines and Reference Series, OECD Publishing, p. 58.
[9] *AMISOM Media Monitoring*, 'Mogadishu Fire Department Chief Resigns over Bakara Inferno', 7 March 2017.
[10] World Population Review, 'Population of Cities in Somalia (2018)', <http://worldpopulationreview.com/countries/somalia-population/cities/>, accessed 31 January 2018.

zones was estimated at 92,618 IDPs and 6,565 economic migrants.[11] Factors contributing to these numbers include two decades of conflict, easy access to weapons, internal displacement prompted by drought and conflict in Mogadishu's neighbouring South-Central zone, high fertility rates, rapid demographic growth, land and water disputes, and, arguably, the lack of formal and accountable government structures willing to spend international humanitarian aid appropriately or collect the taxes needed to fund basic forms of security and development.[12] Consequently, most of the city's inhabitants experience uncertainty and insecurity; many not only feel unsafe, but also cannot access clean water, let alone employment, medical aid or education, and malnutrition is common. The lot of those in Mogadishu's IDP camps may be more extreme, but most of its inhabitants are to a degree vulnerable. Terrorism adds urgency to this picture, and does so indiscriminately, but it does not alter the overall picture. Even so, it affects Mogadishu's poorer residents disproportionately; internationals know that they will be evacuated if the situation becomes too dangerous, and receive medical care if injured, but local people will not.

Security is much improved compared with three or four years ago, and a relatively successful city security plan has since been developed. It is true that the FGS and regional authorities, which barely function at the best of times, effectively cease to operate once tensions increase, as in the run-up to the delayed 2016 elections. But community initiatives to report suspicious incidents to the authorities can still be identified, with a significant example on 17 January 2017, when several NISA troops were killed after storming a house in Waberi district suspected of producing counterfeit US dollars.[13] The fact that thousands of fake dollars were impounded and several arrests made is not important (Somalia is a leading producer of counterfeit dollars). What matters is that the operation took place in Waberi, home to the city's most successful

---

[11]   REACH, 'IDP Assessment in Mogadishu', 22 February 2016; ReliefWeb, 'Daynile IDP Settlements Overview', January 2016, <http://reliefweb.int/sites/reliefweb.int/files/resources/reach_som_mogadishu_factsheet_daynile_settlements_january2016_0.pdf>, accessed 4 September 2016.

[12]   On 4 April 2017, Farmajo's finance minister announced the introduction of an income tax of between 6 and 12 per cent. He aims to raise around $267 million, or 60 per cent of the country's budget of $270 million, with donors expected to meet the deficit. His ability to implement the announcement is open to question, not least because most such schemes are revenue-raising schemes for vested interests. See *AMISOM Daily Media Monitoring*, 'Income Tax Shoots up as Finance Minister ups Domestic Borrowing', 5 April 2017.

[13]   *AMISOM Daily Media Monitoring*, 'NISA Seizes Counterfeit Dollars and Arrests Kingpins', 17 January 2017; see also Goobjoog News, 'NISA Seizes Counterfeit Dollars and Arrests Kingpins', 17 January 2017, <http://goobjoog.com/english/nisa-seizes-counterfeit-dollars-arrests-kingpins/>, accessed 17 January 2017

neighbourhood-watch scheme, and NISA's 'detectives' arrested the suspects in a covert operation following tips from locals.[14] The incident concerned counterfeiting, rather than terrorism, and the residents reported it to NISA, rather than the police, but this case confirms residents' willingness to contact the authorities, while suggesting that formal and informal responses to insecurity and crime are understood as forming part of a coherent response. It also suggests that effectiveness – or 'performance'[15] – is prized even when the agency concerned is feared or distrusted, a fact commonly agreed among internationals and Somali officials. A similar response occurred on 7 May 2017, when a joint police and NISA force retrieved a cache of weapons in Bondheere district following a tip-off from residents.[16]

This chapter offers an overview of the ways Mogadishu's inhabitants manage their environment. It should be noted at the outset that this overview is informed mainly by city officials and officers.[17] It focuses on the neighbourhood-watch scheme found in Waberi district. The chapter looks first at security provision in the districts before noting the international rationale for prioritising police–community engagement and the community policing that is thought to improve it.

Mogadishu's Policing Providers

Low-level security provision presents a complex picture. Officially, the main providers of everyday street-level policing are the SPF, backed by AMISOM and district commissioners' militia; although militiamen may sometimes also be police.

---

[14] The account in *Shabelle News* of the raid refers to NISA soldiers, rather than detectives, but categorisation means little and police are commonly referred to as 'policemen-soldiers'. *Shabelle News*, 'One Dead, as NISA Storms Suspected House in Capital', 17 January 2017.

[15] Performance theory argues that the effective performance of government agencies increases people's trust and confidence in public institutions. See Geert Bouckaert et al., 'Identity Vs. Performance: An Overview of Theories Explaining Trust in Government', Institut voor der Overheit and Katholieke Universiteit Leuven, 2002; Maarten Van Craen and Wesley G Skogan, 'Differences and Similarities in the Explanation of Ethnic Minority Groups' Trust in Police', *European Journal of Criminology* (Vol. 12, No. 3, 2015), pp. 300–23.

[16] *Shabelle News*, 'Somali Forces Seize IEDs in Mogadishu Sweep', 8 May 2017.

[17] This reflects the fact that it is easier for internationals to speak to senior officers and officials in the regional administration than to people living in Waberi's streets. For an emphasis on the 'vernacular understandings' of the poor and excluded, see Robin Luckham, 'Whose Violence, Whose Security? Can Violence Reduction and Security Work for Poor, Excluded and Vulnerable People?', *Peacebuilding* (Vol. 5, No. 2, 2017), pp. 99–117.

The SPF is more effective and professional than it used to be. Members of the SPF now wear police uniforms, the SPF is reputed by the international community to have integrated several clans into its ranks and its officers are theoretically vetted, registered, trained and paid by the international community. In addition, the SPF was relatively effective in the run-up to the presidential elections, managing to maintain order at polling stations, whereas SNA troops used militia to influence voters in favour of parliamentary candidates close to then-President Hassan Sheikh Mohamud.[18] Despite this, the SPF has been infiltrated by clan paramilitaries and Al-Shabaab sympathisers, and its role is more flexible than international models advocate. SPF officers may be present in markets and near significant buildings, but their approach is defensive, with patrolling considered undesirable or incomprehensible, if not suicidal. This is not unusual: AMISOM's heavily armed police units may patrol parts of Mogadishu, but many officers in more volatile or violent societies are reluctant to leave their stations. NISA's security interests ensure that it has a presence in the districts, although its agents do not address everyday crime and community safety issues. Consequently, when residents need help they look first to the various militias of the different district commissioners or they seek protection from their clan.[19]

From an international perspective, the overall picture is fluid and untidy, yet the various elements form a coherent and locally acceptable whole, offering a range of options that suits, rather than undermines, the position – and legitimacy – of the government and regional authorities; it is not as unacceptable to Somalis as is sometimes thought.[20] Nevertheless, many people regard all security forces as a threat, rather than a source of potential security. Men in police or national army uniforms are feared, while AMISOM is perceived to be responsible for a number of deaths. When, during his research, Adam Yusuf Egal asked his Mogadishu respondents about AMISOM's record, several referred to a *Daily Nation Kenya* YouTube video entitled 'Amisom Kills More Civilians than Al-Shabaab: UN', which said that the Somali police and army killed 55 civilians during the last four months of 2016, while AMISOM killed 37.[21]

---

[18] *Indian Ocean Newsletter*, 'Army Under Pressure', Issue 1441, 23 December 2016.
[19] Menkhaus, 'Non-State Security Providers and Political Formation in Somalia', pp. 23–25.
[20] *Ibid.*, p. 6. See also Alex de Waal, *The Real Politics of the Horn of Africa: Money, War and the Business of Power* (Cambridge: Polity, 2015), pp. 110–11, 124–26, 128–29.
[21] *Daily Nation*, 'Amisom Kills more Civilians than Al-Shabaab – UN', 18 January 2017, <http://www.nation.co.ke/video/1951480-3522110-3md90xz/_green>, accessed 18 January 2017.

The video concludes that AMISOM and the Somali army together killed 92 civilians, whereas Al-Shabaab killed 91.

In theory, AMISOM's police units and individual officers play a positive role in influencing both the SPF's local security practices and the community's response to them. AMISOM has introduced a number of community policing sensitisation campaigns and projects designed to improve not only police standards, but also police–community relations at the district level. Officially, such projects are intended to collect crime-related information, although no attention is paid publicly as to how the material might be managed. In practice, the success of the projects depends on the expertise and enthusiasm of individual AMISOM officers, with most of those featured in news stories coming from Ghana, Nigeria and Uganda. By all accounts, residents receive the projects enthusiastically, although the sustainability of the initial response is open to question. There has been no follow-up.

Community Policing

The engagement on which policing projects and long-term stability depend is framed by AMISOM and donors in terms of democratic ideals such as cooperation, partnership and, most notably, community, rather than – as is more realistic – the political economy of policing and clan-based networks.[22] Even so, the term 'community' is difficult to avoid, not least because donors and researchers evidently find comfort in the cooperation and harmony associated with community symbolism.[23] It is therefore used here descriptively, referring to the inhabitants of specific neighbourhoods or districts.

One reason why 'community' is hard to avoid is that donor projects on security and justice are typically framed in terms of 'community policing', a controversial notion which can be defined as a philosophy or ideal that promotes policing as a shared endeavour in which police and communities work together to address crime and disorder. European donors regard it as a desirable organisational strategy or philosophy whereby police respond to local requirements. It is also understood as marking a shift away from the professional model of policing, with its emphasis on technical expertise and bureaucratic command structures, towards more consultative, trust-based problem-solving strategies.

---

[22]   Alice Hills, 'Is There Anybody There? Police, Communities and Communications Technology in Hargeisa', *Stability: International Journal of Security and Development* (Vol. 6, No. 1, 2017).
[23]   Mark Findlay and Uglješa Zvekić, *Alternative Policing Styles: Cross-Cultural Perspectives* (Deventer: Kluwer, 1993), p. 32.

Alternatively, it is understood as including problem-oriented policing, which proposes that policing should address underlying community problems. The OECD DAC's *Handbook on Security Sector Reform*, for instance, states that police are responsible for increasing 'trust between the police and the public' and developing 'partnerships to detect and prevent crime and increase community safety'.[24] In other words, community policing is used as an aspirational goal, rather than as a precise category.

The result is conceptual confusion about the operational direction of policing, with understanding ranging from 'policing the community' to 'communities policing the police'.[25] But in Africa community policing is always about managing the community. Donor definitions may emphasise joint problem-solving, service, diversity and accountability, but the politically and functionally successful forms of community policing in countries such as Nigeria and Ethiopia require communities to take responsibility for their own security and feed information to the police.[26] There is also policy-relevant confusion because community policing reflects donors' belief that police can be agents for social change; as Mark Findlay and Ugliesa Zvekić note, donors are preoccupied with making policing more relevant in its social context, rather than merely improving its crime-control capacity.[27] Even when this is not the case (the EU advisers referred to in Chapter IV focused on developing the Somaliland police's crime-control capacity to improve crime prevention and local security), community policing means whatever the speaker concerned wants it to mean. Findlay and Zvekić cut through the confusion by defining community policing as a 'selective process of communication and accountability',[28] and this is the understanding adopted here. Their insight that the 'interactions of interest, power and authority' distinguishing 'the structures and functions of police work' should be viewed as 'constructed around expectations for policing within a given cultural, political and

---

[24] OECD DAC, *OECD DAC Handbook on Security System Reform (SSR): Supporting Security and Justice*, 2007, p. 163.

[25] Mike Brogden and Preeti Nijhar, *Community Policing: National and International Models and Approaches* (Cullompton: Willan, 2005); Lisa Denney, 'Securing Communities? Redefining Community Policing to Achieve Results', ODI, 2005; Hills, 'Is There Anybody There?'.

[26] Alice Hills, 'Partnership Policing: Is it Relevant in Kano, Nigeria?', *Criminology & Criminal Justice* (Vol. 14, No. 1, 2014), pp. 8–24; Lisa Denney, 'Securing Communities for Development: Community Policing in Ethiopia's Amhara National Regional State', ODI, 2013.

[27] Findlay and Zvekić, *Alternative Policing*, p. 33.

[28] *Ibid.*

situational context' is especially helpful,[29] supplementing that of Cooper-Knock and Owen on the utility of police for local people.[30] In other words, police and communities ideally develop a pragmatic working relationship that builds on a locally acceptable understanding of their respective roles regarding the management of low-level forms of insecurity and disorder.

Such an understanding prioritises people's need for physical safety and the protection of property, rather than trust and cooperation. It is true that Somali society depends on trust,[31] but it is also characterised by high levels of suspicion which undermine capacity-building projects. The part played by discretion and initiative in this has yet to be investigated, but for now, the use of discretion is more evident than initiative. Indeed, discretion, or the tempering of strict rules for policy or operational reasons, is a feature of Somalia's legally plural society and an essential and legitimate element in policing world wide.[32] Further, Somali notions of what it means to be police requires a flexible approach to policing that acknowledges the importance of customary, traditional and Islamic law.[33] Entrepreneurial ingenuity drives many aspects of Somali life and there is no obvious reason why policing provision should be exempt from this.

Despite this, the notion of the police working with the public, officials and agencies to address community safety is popular among donors. Nevertheless, most such examples emphasise the one-way nature of community–police relations, with the onus for local security placed on residents. Ethiopia, for instance, values the effect community policing has on improving social control, whereas the model promoted by the UK in Nigeria emphasises community mobilisation and partnership.[34] Meanwhile, AMISOM emphasises the security benefits of community policing and its potential to build closer relationships between the police and the public:

> We have decided to roll out community policing because ... it is the best way of fighting criminal activities in communities. We have decided to involve the community so that they work with the police to identify their own problems; they coordinate with the police and fight the criminal activities within themselves.[35]

---

[29] *Ibid.*, p. 6.
[30] Cooper-Knock and Owen, 'Between Vigilantism and Bureaucracy'.
[31] Neil Carrier, *Little Mogadishu* (London: Hurst, 2016), pp. 85–89, 171–77.
[32] Findlay and Zvekić, *Alternative Policing*, p. 21.
[33] Alice Hills, 'What is Policeness? On Being Police in Somalia', *British Journal of Criminology* (Vol. 54, No. 5, 2014), pp. 765–83.
[34] Denney, 'Securing Communities for Development'.
[35] *Coastweek.com*, 'Somali Security Build Mogadishu Community Policing Partnerships', May 2014.

And many Mogadishu residents accept that they are largely responsible for local security. For example, in the summer of 2014, AMISOM held a meeting in Wadajir, the city's most populous district, at which the district commissioner promoted a toll-free line, 888, for sharing crime-related information. He stressed that the public should embrace the initiative, which would, he said, facilitate community policing: 'Community policing is important for the peace stabilization since our country has come from war. So our country is not as we wanted. So we are trying to get the peace and just restore the peace and we are rebuilding our country. We need to return our communities as they were in 1980'[36] – that is, when the city was safe.

The strength of the commissioner's sentiments may reflect the relative security of Wadijir, but they are also common. When Egal asked what community policing meant to ten respondents who had lived in Mogadishu for ten years and had at least a secondary education, they all replied that it was not widely known but they had heard of it and thought that it referred to the relationship between police and community. Some said that it exists in name only, and is not something that exists in – or works for – all districts, while others thought it was an initiative driven by donors or AMISOM.[37] This is to an extent true, with AMISOM's police projects receiving the most publicity.

AMISOM's Police Projects
In February 2016, AMISOM's police component and the SPF met with 150 residents of Hodan district (of note because it is home to Mogadishu's khat centre and Bakara Market's fruit and vegetable section) to discuss ideas for keeping the district safe. Hodan was also the site of fierce fighting between Al-Shabaab, AMISOM and the Transitional FGS from 2010 to 2014.

The meeting (described by AMISOM as a 'sensitisation meeting') was part of an AMISOM community policing initiative designed to improve trust in – and between – the SPF and AMISOM, as well as between AMISOM and the community.[38] As Hodan's police commander stressed, AMISOM has:

> [P]ut in a lot of time and effort to help us. We have worked hard at improving relations with the population, the administration and Police. We are now working to improve civic education in order to improve our work and security through partnership with the public,

---

[36] *Ibid.*
[37] Egal, 'Police Corruption, Radicalization and Terrorist Attacks in Mogadishu'.
[38] *Coastweek.com*, 'Somali Security Build Mogadishu Community Policing Partnerships'.

administration AMISOM police and Somali police. The situation is improving.[39]

In Hodan, as in similar meetings in Warta Nabada and Hamar Weyne, AMISOM, the SPF and the district administration discussed security concerns with local people and, where possible, identified 'homegrown solutions to crime and related concerns'. According to AMISOM's public information officer, this was done with the goal of building public trust in law enforcement agencies, and the approach was adopted because in fighting crime, it is:

> not enough to eliminate the criminal elements within our communities … we [therefore] embarked on the sensitization drive to educate the members, to cooperate with the security forces, to come up and join hands in fighting crime.[40]

Statements urging engagement and working together form a large part in such meetings, as does a strong emphasis on security. Thus, Hodan's deputy district commissioner in charge of social affairs stressed that the police and the public should work together because 'it is the only way we can realize development and our people can take advantage of the stability to improve their business and life'.[41] Other speakers stressed that 'what matters most in life is security'; 'if you are not safe there is no life' – and the implication was that community policing would deliver this.[42]

Given AMISOM's use of the term 'community policing' and the importance of gathering information from communities for Mogadishu's city security plan, questions arise about the significance of community policing, and its relationship to neighbourhood-watch schemes. Anecdotally, the term 'community policing' is rarely used outside AMISOM and donor circles, but it is nonetheless relevant here because it conveys the notion that communities can help to protect themselves by reporting crime and suspicious incidents to the police – by reporting information that could prevent crime and, more importantly, by providing the actionable intelligence needed by the city's security plan.

Ken Menkhaus argues that Somali community policing has been designed to manage and prevent criminal violence, rather than terrorism,[43] but neither the SPF nor donors such as the UK and the US distinguish sharply between the two. Also, as AMISOM's statements imply,

---

[39] *Ibid.*

[40] *Ibid.*

[41] *Ibid.*

[42] *Ibid.*

[43] Ken Menkhaus, 'Can Community Policing Combat Al-Shabaab?', IPI Global Observatory, 2014.

the idea behind today's approach to community policing is that it results in the development of neighbourhood reporting groups that cooperate to inhibit the activities of both criminals and terrorists. And this has long been acceptable in Mogadishu, as has ambiguity between the two functions. In July 2011, the Police Advisory Committee's (PAC) 'Monthly Report on the Activities of the Somali Police Force' emphasised the SPF's role in counterterrorism and counterinsurgency, rather than civilian policing, and routinely referred to officers as 'policemen-soldiers'.[44] It is true that the advisory committee, a small group of educated and, in some cases, politically ambitious Somalis, provided what it thought would appeal to donors such as the UN. Also, like all the committee's reports, the one from July divides police activities into operations intended 'to enhance community safety' and 'street patrolling as part of wider counter terrorism efforts'.[45] Yet it also reflects the ways that local-level policing is based on a tactical and flexible adaptation of current needs and resources, legacy issues and international approaches to community policing.

SPF and Community Policing
The SPF's website takes an orthodox understanding of community policing, which is presented in terms of principles such as policing by consent, police and community working together, and policing tailored to meet community needs and priorities.[46] The SPF has had a dedicated community policing unit since 2011 (led initially by former diaspora Lieutenant Colonel Zakia Hussein), and its website defines community policing as 'both a philosophy (a way of thinking) and an organizational strategy … that allows the police and community to work together to solve problems of crime and insecurity. Ultimately, the objective is to isolate criminals and thus ensure a 'safe and secure environment for all citizens'.[47] Its policing practices are said to be based on communities making decisions about their own security, and to be underpinned by long-term partnerships between communities and the police. Indeed, a spokesman at a 2015 event to welcome a 150-strong special police force trained to fight terrorism praised the new unit while emphasising the FGS's plans to strengthen the working relationship between the police and the public by creating a community policing and public relations unit: 'The police is the community and the community is the police … This is the slogan we

---

[44] Police Advisory Committee (PAC), 'Report on the Somali Police Force, July 2011'.
[45] *Ibid*.
[46] Somaligov.net, 'Community Policing', <http://www.police.somaligov.net/Community%20Policing%20.html>, accessed 25 January 2018.
[47] *Ibid*

operate under. We have put up billboards on some roads that detail how the police and the public work together'.[48]

It is easy to be cynical about such statements, yet the author's conversations with police officers and observations at Benadir's police headquarters in July 2016 suggest that some senior officers are genuinely convinced that, when suitably adjusted for local conditions, community policing offers the best way to collect information and, importantly, to make their working lives safer; as Ian Loader and Neil Walker note, policing is oriented to answer the question, 'How well ordered is my immediate environment?'[49] And this can mean the environment of the police officer as well as those the officer is tasked to protect. Indeed, the suggestion here is that the police and the public share an understanding of their respective roles in managing low-level insecurity, while collecting information that could potentially benefit their community. The rest of this chapter explores how this understanding is put into practice.

Intelligence-Gathering at the Local Level

Before 2015, Mogadishu's formal security plans were top-down products that failed to deliver on their promises. However, the new Mogadishu city security plan differs from these old plans in that it acknowledges the role played by the city's districts in intelligence collection and street-level security. It not only includes a recommendation to base the city's response on the reporting structure used by the then mayor's neighbourhood-watch scheme, but it also adopts neighbourhood watch as a primary pillar for both Mogadishu's security strategy and its policing development.

Significantly, the mayor's scheme draws on Somali practices used during the 1970s and 2000s, rather than on international models of community policing. In the 1970s, President Barre introduced a form of community policing called *hamuunta* or 'directing the people' (that is, connecting people to the state) which was used to manage groups or clans that he saw as a threat (it was linked to the military in terms of its reporting mechanisms and control methods). More recently, in 2002–03 civil society organisations developed a coordinated and structured community security system based on neighbourhoods. Known as 'neighbourhood watch' and funded by monthly contributions from each household, the scheme used security committees and armed community

---

[48] Khalid Yusuf, 'Somali Federal Government Forms Counter-Terrorism Police Unit', *Horseed Media*, 7 January 2015, <https://horseedmedia.net/2015/01/07/somali-federal-government-forms-counterterrorism-police-unit/>, accessed 9 January 2015.
[49] Ian Loader and Neil Walker, *Civilizing Security* (Cambridge: CUP, 2005), p. 205.

police officers to monitor and manage crime. Selection and training followed agreed rules while real-time security developments were monitored using a popular radio programme called 'Hodi Hodi?' ('May I come in?'). Reputedly, this initiative was very successful, but it faded after the formation of the Transitional FGS in 2004 encouraged the expectation that it would provide security, and it was not until 2013 that Benadir's regional administration launched the programme that is the precursor of today's neighbourhood-watch schemes. Called the 'Fostering Neighbourhood and Social Integration Programme', it enlisted local people to prevent terrorist attacks and crime, and today's scheme builds on this.

It is true to say that Mogadishu's neighbourhood-watch groups have for many years been little more than vigilantes, clan-based militia or protection groups designed to manage criminal violence rather than ordinary crime, let alone terrorism. But much has changed since 2015 and the neighbourhood-watch scheme is the most locally acceptable, sustainable and value-for-money approach to urban security currently available in the city. Additionally, it provides an entrance into the city security plan's approach to intelligence collection while offering general insights into the relationship between counterterrorism and social cohesion and community safety and, ultimately, development. Further, it is the first example of a government-led system for systematically collating security information and intelligence. It provides a reality check on claims made for international assistance and development aid by showing that bottom-up policing initiatives are more meaningful than top-down projects while emphasising that the critical variable in cities such as Mogadishu is physical security today, rather than in the future.

Neighbourhood watch is only one of several policing projects designed to rally residents, but it is arguably the scheme that is most embedded in Somali society. The mayor's scheme was promoted at the same time as the Ministry of Internal Security introduced a 'Know your neighbour' campaign and AMISOM's police component rolled out a version designed to build policing partnerships and thus contribute to the African Union's understanding of community policing.[50] AMISOM's scheme, for instance, which is widely known as the 'ten household monitoring system', requires one resident to take charge of ten houses and report on the inhabitants' activities every morning. Residents also attend Sunday meetings (in large numbers) at which crime and security-related concerns are discussed.

Waberi's neighbourhood-watch scheme also consists of a structured approach to gathering intelligence at the neighbourhood level but,

---

[50] *Ibid.*

crucially, it is locally driven and seemingly more attractive to both residents and the SPF's local commander. Designed to mobilise the community, it builds on the appointment of community representatives, who are responsible for recording sightings of suspicious individuals, vehicles and weapons. The results are fed to a neighbourhood team – composed of ordinary residents – that collates and analyses the information to create a picture of security-relevant activities, before it is passed to agencies such as the police, the Ministry of Internal Security and NISA, with the SPF acting as a filter between neighbourhood watch and the city security plan's JIMC. The result is a process linking neighbourhood watch to the city's district commissioners, the regional administration, and the SPF's Community Policing and Public Relations Division.

Mogadishu's scheme is also different to those found elsewhere in the region. In Somaliland, for example, neighbourhood watch refers to night-time protection groups or community police (the terms are used synonymously) comprising local youths, businessmen, elders and women, who respond to alarms or alerts. Established in collaboration with the Somaliland police, districts in towns such as Hargeisa and Burao pay their community police a small sum of money each month to safeguard their property at night.[51] There are problems associated with this form of policing in that people fear that the groups are infiltrated by Al-Shabaab or criminals; but for most it is an acceptable solution. No-one expects police officers to respond quickly, least of all at night. In contrast, Mogadishu's neighbourhood watch is broadly based.

The discussion here focuses on the neighbourhood-watch scheme in the strategically important district of Waberi because it is the most developed – and successful – of the various initiatives, and is to some extent a showpiece, with its processes now used across a range of districts. It is valuable for its granular details, which offer insight into how security actually functions at the local level, and what residents do to feel safe.

Keeping Waberi Safe

Located to the northeast of Aden Adde International Airport, and with the main road from the airport to the presidential palace running through it, Waberi is a densely populated district of some 19,250 inhabitants from non-Somali ethnic minorities (the Benadiri) living in approximately 3,850

---

[51] Small Arms Survey, 'Between State and Non-state: Somaliland's Emerging Security Order', in Small Arms Survey 2012 (Cambridge: CUP, 2012), pp. 163–67, <www.smallarmssurvey.org/fileadmin/.../Small-Arms-Survey-2012-Chapter-05-EN.pdf>, accessed 4 March 2013.

houses laid out in a grid system. The district includes ten informal camps housing 15,000 internally displaced persons.

Waberi's neighbourhood-watch scheme is Somali-driven and subject to mayoral politics, although for much of 2014–16 it was advised by several former senior UK police officers and supported by the British Embassy as a means to increase counterterrorism-relevant reporting to the regional administration and the police.[52] In practice, this meant that the UK supported neighbourhood watch to enhance the police's role in counterterrorism and thereby offset NISA's influence, while improving communication between the FGS, district commissioners and local people. But, from the perspective of Waberi's residents, the scheme was about improving community safety and cooperation, and minimising Al-Shabaab's influence.

Neighbourhood-Watch Scheme

Best imagined as a pyramid, the neighbourhood watch builds up from 'street committee' volunteers, representing groups of ten houses, to 'neighbourhood committee' volunteers, representing five street committees (50 households), to sector committees, representing four neighbourhood committees (200 households), to ward committees, representing four sectors (800 households), to suburb committees, representing four ward committees (1,800 households), and finally to a district committee, representing four suburbs (7,000 households). All posts are filled by volunteers, the majority of whom are women (polygamy means that many men will have, say, four wives, each of whom will have a separate house).

Waberi's 700 volunteers are organised by six 'fieldworkers', each of whom receives US$75 (AMISOM deducts US$5 for administration). The groups meet every morning and record their observations on paper – for example, suspicious individuals are passed to the neighbourhood-watch office. The information is photocopied before being transferred to Excel spreadsheets – in English – by seventeen inputters, each of whom has a desktop computer supplied by the UK. The office's single networked computer connects to a cloud server. Once a week, a district security

---

[52] In summer 2016, budget constraints led to the scheme's funding being reallocated to complementary projects associated with the city security plan. The focus could shift again if Whitehall's agenda changes. But budgetary issues are not the only reason for the scheme's potential survivability; international aid (and money in particular) makes it a target for politicians. On 6 April 2017, Farmajo replaced the mayor responsible for developing the original scheme who was in turn replaced in January 2018, and it is not yet clear what the current mayor will do.

committee consisting of the district commissioner and the SPF and NISA district commanders meets.

At first glance, the scheme looks unsustainably labour intensive and complicated. Moreover, the longevity of the equipment used is unknown, and the production of daily reports in English requires hours of painstaking work. Yet labour is not an issue and the equipment and resources needed are modest. Three days' training for 700 people costs $4,100, and office furniture, computers and photocopiers cost just $6,600.

Nevertheless, the neighbourhood-watch scheme – and the plans to roll it out across Mogadishu's seventeen districts – requires international support. The support needed is both minimal and cost-effective, yet donors, which can spend thousands of dollars on anti-radicalisation projects, have refused to buy chlorine to disinfect the cholera-breeding stagnant water alongside the funded football field.[53] Similarly, the scheme's offices are in poor condition and frequent flooding prevents the installation of promised equipment.

By the end of 2015, 700 people had been trained in the most appropriate ways to keep Waberi safe, in the role of the SPF, and how to record relevant information. Literacy levels are low, so training was delivered by using singing and acting performances and small-group explanations involving residents, police officers and district officials. The success of such methods in improving morale, social cohesion and street-level security was implied by the district commissioner's request that her leadership team be included in the programme. More tellingly, improved security led to house prices and rental costs in the district increasing.

Comprehensive and Sustainable Security

A key feature of Waberi's neighbourhood-watch scheme is that it integrates counterterrorism and everyday community safety issues in a way that is politically sanctioned, locally acceptable, and which promotes reconciliation and development. Every morning representatives from the locality meet to identify health, welfare and safety concerns, as well as suspicious vehicles or visitors. In addition to the effective way in which information is collected, sifted and fed to the city security plan, Waberi's scheme suggests that the empirical and analytical boundaries between counterterrorism (as an instance of traditional security) and residents' everyday concerns (as an expression of soft security) are porous, with their precise delineation depending on context.

---

53 Author interview with UK adviser, Mogadishu, 28 July 2016.

This is not to suggest that the relationship with counterterrorism is politically unproblematic for the neighbourhood-watch scheme. Indeed, the link to counterterrorism leaves the scheme at risk of being tainted in two specific ways, both of which may lead to it being deprived of donor resources.

First, neighbourhood watch's collection of intelligence encourages international critics to conflate its work with that of a controversial Mogadishu-based NGO with similar concerns: Somali Women Against Violent Extremism (SWAVE). Like neighbourhood watch, SWAVE is Somali-driven, but its work is more sharply focused on counterterrorism. SWAVE receives no international funding and draws on a network of ten women in each district who are tasked with collecting counterterrorism-related intelligence, which is then fed into the Joint Operations Coordination Center. SWAVE is best understood as performing a complementary role that works to the advantage of neighbourhood watch – it focuses on counterterrorism in a way that neighbourhood watch cannot and should not.

Second, associating neighbourhood-watch's work with that of SWAVE lays neighbourhood watch open to censure from, for instance, the EU and UNSOM, which then block funding and support. Some international critics argue that neighbourhood watch should not be supported because those reporting incidents may be subject to intimidation, especially if they are believed to be spies (one such case resulted in a woman's death in 2015). But, in practice, the risk of neighbourhood watch putting local people at risk is relatively low. Neighbourhood watch's everyday business is concerned with reporting the presence of suspicious strangers or vehicles and incidents arising from poverty and unemployment such as robbery, which illustrates the ways in which residents try to manage both terrorism and everyday street-level threats. Additionally, neighbourhood watch's work involves a modicum of welfare support. For example, women street-cleaners are given a bowl of *dhal* (their only meal of the day) for their work – street-cleaning helps to prevent explosives being hidden, which is important as the scheme's acceptability and sustainability requires it to offer practical value to those engaged with it.

The relationship between the types of security associated with counterterrorism and those associated with community safety is clearly significant, although the nature of the interface and the points at which the categorisation shifts are unclear. The unifying role of physical security offers an entrance into these issues, but – from an international perspective – two additional analytical tools also deserve consideration: human or people-centred security, and the security–development nexus. Both are often thought to have analytical potential when applied to societies such as Mogadishu's because they are based on the belief that the security and welfare of the population, as opposed to the security of the state or regime, is more important when considering ways of tackling the predicament confronting the city. Indeed, it has been argued that human security in particular allows for a more accurate assessment of the ways in which actors and institutions in post-conflict environments contribute to or threaten the security of different demographic categories (such as men, women and children), and how the resultant insecurities relate to the roles, responsibilities, practices and organisation of the police.[54] But in practice both lack traction in Mogadishu.

The first term, human security, was popularised by the UN Development Programme in the early 1990s at a time when the end of the Cold War refocused attention on the complexity and interrelatedness of security threats, ranging from ethnic conflict to poverty and climate change. It was promoted by officials from mid-ranking countries such as Canada, Japan and Norway,[55] and debated by researchers in journals such as *Security Dialogue*.[56] However, the relevance of the term to volatile and insecure societies such as Mogadishu's has yet to be rigorously assessed. Definitional issues exacerbate the problem. Human security may, for example, be understood as a descriptive notion that prioritises the welfare and safety of the individual over that of the state. Alternatively, it is sometimes defined as an aspiration or goal referring to freedom from violence and from the fear of violence.[57] Others dismiss the concept as merely the latest in a long line of neologisms.[58] It is a notion, rather than a systematically developed concept, that has nevertheless been subject to significant conceptual and political stretching.[59] Admittedly, most of the issues incorporated into it are present in Mogadishu, from organised crime, acute poverty, inequality, and the absence of health and education facilities to climate change. But human security's emphasis on the

---

[54] NMBU, 'Community-Based Policing and Post-Conflict Police Reform', unpublished proposal for 'EC CALL H2020-FCT-14-2014: Fight against Crime and Terrorism - Topic: Ethical/Societal Dimension Topic 2: Enhancing cooperation between law enforcement agencies & citizens/Community Policing', 2014, p. 15.
[55] See, for example, Lloyd Axworthy, 'Human Security and Global Governance: Putting People First', *Global Governance* (Vol. 7, No. 1, 2010), pp. 19–23.
[56] Ryerson Christie gives an insightful overview of the literature on human security. See Ryerson Christie, 'Critical Voices and Human Security', *Security Dialogue* (Vol. 41, No. 10, 2010), pp. 169–90.
[57] UN Trust Fund for Human Security, 'Human Security in Theory and Practice', 2009, <http://www.un.org/humansecurity/sites/www.un.org.humansecurity/files/human_security_in_theory_and_practice_english.pdf>, accessed 30 September 2014.
[58] Roland Paris, 'Human Security: Paradigm Shift or Hot Air?', *International Security* (Vol. 26, No. 2, 2002), p. 87.
[59] Giovanni Sartori, 'Concept Misinformation in Comparative Politics', *American Political Science Review* (Vol. 64, No. 4, 1970), pp. 1033–53.

importance of population groups such as women or children, rather than the state, undermines its utility in this context. Not only is the state the primary political reference point for the international community, but the individual counts for little in Somalia's clan-based society; powerful men do not care about ordinary people, and the SPF is not organised or designed to address such issues. Also, the activities of Al-Shabaab emphasise that human security's goals can be achieved only when conventional security functions – and the requirement to counter terrorism will always take priority. Consequently, human security cannot act as either a critical analytical tool or empirical linkage in today's Mogadishu. Similar considerations apply to the widely accepted notion of a security–development nexus.

For many donors and NGOs, security and its management is best understood in terms of a security–development nexus whereby security and development are inextricably linked. At the same time as the notion of human security emerged, security and development were progressively conceptualised as mutually reinforcing and a central link sustaining transition from conflict to stabilisation and recovery.[60] The idea of a security–development nexus also reflected the identification of new security concerns focusing on under-development as a source of conflict, crime and instability, rather than on conventional war. This relates to Mogadishu's predicament in that the nexus is anchored in donor-driven issues such as state-building, peacebuilding, security sector reform and social change, although it also incorporates the future-oriented goals that many Waberi residents would like to see applied to their children's lives. But, in practice, Mogadishu's insecurity constrains the ability of donors to operate in the city, let alone influence its power dynamics. Other issues obstructing the applicability of the nexus include the city's inhabitants fragmenting into clan-based categories, its functioning depending on the modicum of security offered by state-based representatives such as NISA, and by everyone's need for physical security today, not in five years' time. Consequently, while it makes analytical sense to explore how the security provided by neighbourhood-watch schemes, the police and militiamen relates to future-oriented goals and processes, notions such as human security and a security–development nexus do not offer a realistic, let alone innovative, way of studying policing in the districts. Assessing the city's security challenges in terms of human security or the security–development nexus is likely to result in inaccurate analysis and incoherent or unrealistic policies.

---

[60] Mark Duffield, *Global Governance and the New Wars: The Merging of Development and Security* (London: Zed Books, 2001), p. 7.

For now, the most striking feature of Waberi's neighbourhood-watch scheme is that it reflects a comprehensive understanding of security in which philosophical issues such as uncertainty, contingency and vulnerability are understood at the level of practical engagement. It is also Somali-driven. Although affected by the regional administration's internecine rivalries, it is supported by the president, the prime minister, the SPF and regional police commissioners, all of whom attend high-profile neighbourhood-watch events. Meanwhile, the SPF cluster commander, who identifies community policing as a primary strand in his strategy for encouraging the common ownership of security issues, bases his policing delivery on a small Waberi police station, providing accommodation to the neighbourhood-watch scheme to ensure a contact point between it, the SPF and the district's residents. Additionally, as the district commissioner noted at a 2016 meeting attended by the district police commander and AMISOM's (police) public information officer, Waberi's good security resulted from not only public support, but also the close working relationship between the SPF and NISA – the latter is informed of anything that happens in the district. And the administration is well connected; unlike the district as a whole, the administration is dominated by the Hawiye-Abgaal sub-clan, with the Hawiye clan the second largest in Somalia after the Darood clan, which helps it to manage local politics. Having said this, anecdotal evidence suggests that belonging to the wrong sub-clan ensures that otherwise admirable NGO activists are prevented from contributing to community initiatives, such as the neighbourhood-watch scheme.

Overall, the neighbourhood-watch scheme's broad appeal helps to ensure that it is sustainable in a way that internationally driven security and policing approaches are not. Sophisticated initiatives such as the Joint Operations Coordination Center may be desirable, but their continued operation depends on the presence of international advisers, whereas this is not the case for the neighbourhood-watch scheme, which reflects Somali experiences and preferences. Rather than representing a repressive mode of surveillance, neighbourhood watch expresses the value Somalis place on social capital and information,[61] neither of which is synonymous with Western-style development.

And neighbourhood-watch schemes produce quantifiable results. Records show that in November 2015 there were 44 arrests attributable to neighbourhood-watch sources, 49 weapons were seized, 41 suspicious persons were targeted, and seventeen suspicious vehicle reports were

---

[61] Menkhaus, 'Community Policing'.

filed, which resulted in actionable intelligence.[62] In March 2016, 2,152 public complaints were received: 1,492 were solved and 660 unsolved (a rate of 31 per cent).[63] In the first three months of 2016, 58 per cent of complainants were women, 34 per cent children, 6 per cent elderly men and women, and 2 per cent men.[64] Typical intelligence reports include a woman member reporting six youths in a suspicious minibus. The police confiscated the bus, found two pistols and AK-47 ammunition, and arrested all six. In another case, an elderly restaurant owner was arrested, along with three youths, after a neighbourhood-watch member reported the four frequently arriving at the restaurant separately late at night or early in the morning. Although these figures are affected by the police's inability to deal with crime, NISA's unwillingness to disclose the results of its investigations, and 80 per cent of ordinary crime being resolved through customary law (*xeer*), no branch of the FGS produces comparable statistics.

Conclusions

Waberi's neighbourhood-watch scheme shows how residents try to make their district safer. It should not be romanticised, but it is a sustainable and locally acceptable project that improves social mobilisation and community safety while helping to produce the actionable intelligence that Benadir's regional administration needs. In other words, it helps to make Mogadishu safer.

---

[62] Author interview with UK adviser, Mogadishu, 17 July 2016.
[63] *Ibid.*
[64] *Ibid.*

IV. ICT FOR COMMUNITY SECURITY

Neighbourhood watch has yet to be implemented throughout Mogadishu's districts, but Waberi's experience shows how successful such schemes can be at mobilising communities and collecting the information and intelligence needed to make the district safer. Nevertheless, police–community relations remain marred by distrust, and the collecting of information, let alone of intelligence, remains a long-standing challenge in a clan-based culture in which family and clan come before crime reporting, and memories of Barre's formidable policing system continue to influence attitudes. Waberi's police station may be a place where residents can engage with officers, but most crime is not reported to the police, and even if it were, few expect the police to respond. Most victims turn first to elders or religious leaders.

Little is known about the police force's attempts to collect information and intelligence, although what exists is probably driven by the need for actionable intelligence on Al-Shabaab, rather than as an aspect of crime prevention or resource allocation. AMISOM and UNSOM provide relevant courses, while donors such as the UK and the US deliver training for criminal intelligence and forensic purposes, which officers say they value because it is proper policing in a way that community policing is not. But such training has limited application because Somali officers do not follow chains of evidence in the way that a European officer might. Indeed, anecdotal and circumstantial reports suggest that many have no understanding of why evidence should be collected.[1] Also, the most valued forms of investigative training are reputedly aligned to the physical coercion style employed by NISA. And this has been true for some years. For example, 2012 saw the introduction of a cash-for-tips scheme that provided a reward of $500 dollars for information relating to the capture of Al-Shabaab leaders and $100 dollars for information on the

---

[1]   Comments based on the author's observations and private conversations in police stations, training colleges and the offices of international organisations in Somaliland, Puntland and Mogadishu, 2011, 2015 and 2016.

whereabouts of low-rank Al-Shabaab officials, but there was no mention of rewards for passing on information on everyday crime.[2] The scheme was also applied to the police, with Somali news site *Dhacdo.com* noting in October 2016 that 'security branches continue to promise monetary awards for police members who either arrest or kill Al-Shabaab assassins'.[3]

A report released by the FGS's predecessor, the Transitional FGS (TFG), in April 2012, stated that the main target of such schemes was Al-Shabaab's leaders and financiers. As a government officer noted at the time, 'both the police and the military needs information relating to the Al-Shabaab militia and their leaders as it is becoming difficult to distinguish people in this busy recovering city, so we are urging the Somali population to work much closer with the authorities'.[4] A popular Mogadishu elder told the *Somalia Report* news network that the government should reward anyone willing to provide information on the whereabouts of leaders of the 'militia' or the location of hidden explosive devices: 'I think everything now is in the hands of the Somali population. It is up to us to either stabilize our country by reporting any suspicious incidents or persons to the authority'.[5] But he admitted that he had not heard of Al-Shabaab leaders being caught by such methods, only of 'fighters who surrendered' for unspecified reasons. Other residents were reported as questioning the programme on the basis that they feared that informants would be reported to Al-Shabaab, who would then punish them. This was sensible because, although the police said that the identities of those cooperating would be kept secret, the chances of this happening were minimal.[6] Revealingly, many of *Somalia Report's* respondents said that it was not hard to find Al-Shabaab officials. According to one Mogadishu-based politician, with the exception of Ahmed Abdi Godane (the emir on whom the US placed a $7-million bounty in June 2012), almost all Al-Shabaab leaders were – and probably still are – easily accessible in the areas they control.[7] Indeed, he said that the project had more to do with propaganda than information-gathering; in other words, it was intended to 'instill [sic] fear in the targeted Al-Shabaab leaders limiting them to intermingle freely with the population they control'. His suspicion that a gulf existed between the public and law

---

[2] US dollars are the preferred currency; see Young Pelton, Nuxurkey and Osman, 'The Police of Somalia, Somaliland, Puntland'.

[3] *AMISOM Media Monitoring*, '20 Arrested in Mogadishu Security Operation', 3 October 2016.

[4] Young Pelton, Nuxurkey and Ozman, 'The Police of Somalia, Somaliland, Puntland'.

[5] *Ibid.*

[6] *Ibid.*

[7] *Ibid.*

enforcement agencies was reinforced when, a month later, *Somalia Report* discovered that no Al-Shabaab leader had been arrested in Mogadishu, with or without the reward scheme. The concluding paragraph of *Somalia Report's* investigative article provides the best evidence of the SPF's passive approach to collecting information: 'The Somali Police can be reached', it says, at 'Villa Somalia, Mogadishu, Somalia 55454, Phone: 2525424640, Fax: 2525424640, E-Mail: webmaster@police.somaligov.net'.

Whether the situation has changed fundamentally since 2012 is open to question, but the continued lack of government infrastructure, combined with the physical vulnerability of officers and the number of Al-Shabaab sympathisers in the police and districts, suggests that it has not. Indeed, with the exception of several station commanders who are sympathetic to community policing, the neighbourhood-watch scheme's successful operation owes little to the police. Support for this interpretation can be found in the fact that Waberi's residents report counterfeiting operations to NISA's 'detectives' rather than to the SPF's criminal investigations department. Nevertheless, it is clear from numerous OCVP surveys that in an ideal world people would like the police to be their primary security provider.[8] They may distrust the police, and no-one expects officers to respond to calls for assistance, but there is nonetheless a willingness to visit police stations when necessary and a degree of understanding for the position that the police find themselves in as a result of insufficient resources and training.[9] As ever, there is a disconnection between people's stated preference and actual behaviour, yet many appear to have no fundamental objection to providing information to police.

What, then, might improve communication? On what does police–community engagement depend? These are the key questions to be addressed. The Anglo-American literature unequivocally identifies trust and legitimacy as the key factors affecting relations and engagement.[10] However, developing trust is problematic in a society as volatile as Somalia's, characterised as it is by suspicion and distrust. Admittedly, business, political and social relations are built on clan-based trust, yet the clan is itself a flexible construct that can be used to advance specific goals, strengthening or undermining trust in the SPF and the government

---

[8] OCVP, 'Mogadishu 2014: Central Zone, Conflict and Security Assessment Report', pp. 16–17; OCVP, 'Safety and Security Report'.
[9] OCVP, 'Mogadishu 2014', pp. xii–xiii.
[10] Jason Sunshine and Tom Tyler, 'The Role of Procedural Justice and Legitimacy in Shaping Public Support for Policing', *Law and Society Review* (Vol. 37, No. 3, 2002), pp. 513–48; Justice Tankabe, 'Viewing Things Differently: The Dimensions of Public Perceptions of Police Legitimacy', *Criminology* (Vol. 51, No. 1, 2013), pp. 103–35.

it is thought to represent.[11] Also, identifying trust as the critical issue might be misleading. Although Anglo-American research and experience focuses on it, other strands of comparative literature suggest that effectiveness and efficiency may be equally important.[12]

As Chapter II notes, performance theory suggests that it is the actions of government agencies that influence trust in the agency concerned,[13] and this certainly appears to be the case in Muslim cities such as Kano, the biggest city in Nigeria's Islamic north – and Kano's experience is more relevant here than New York's or Belgium's. Thus, the Nigeria Police Force has been relatively successful in managing the complex, competitive and legally plural environment found in Kano,[14] but this owes nothing to the trust-based, networked operations identified in analyses of policing in liberal democracies such as the UK.[15] Indeed, the suspicion and volatility characterising Kano's environment requires that the regular police must be backed by the paramilitary Police Mobile Force (PMF), which was established as an anti-riot squad capable of countering communal disturbances, banditry, insurrection and militants when regular police cannot cope. Only regular officers can join the PMF, but the two are visibly distinct: the PMF wear khaki and black uniforms made of military-quality cloth that takes razor-sharp creases, whereas regular police wear black and blue uniforms which do not. Significantly, the PMF receives special public order training, which is popularly thought to make them 'agile, alert, serious, colourful and attractive' to a public concerned by Kano's crime and insecurity.[16] This, combined with their operational effectiveness, encourages people to regard them with respect and confidence, as well as distrust and fear; they act quickly if brutally, and are called on for help by victims in distress during, for example, armed robberies or gang fights. In other words, the PMF relies on coercion and effectiveness, rather than trust, to achieve its aims, and most local people tolerate or acquiesce in this. Arguably, this approach is more relevant in

---

[11] Compare Neil Carrier, *Little Mogadishu: Eastleigh, Nairobi's Global Somali Hub* (London: Hurst, 2016).

[12] Tankabe, 'Viewing Things Differently'.

[13] Geert Bouckaert et al., 'Identity vs Performance: An Overview of Theories Explaining Trust in Government', Catholic University Leuven, 2002.

[14] Hills, 'Policing a Plurality of Worlds: The Nigeria Police in Metropolitan Kano'.

[15] See Alice Hills, 'Partnership Policing: Is it Relevant in Kano, Nigeria?', *Criminology and Criminal Justice* (Vol. 14, No. 1, 2014), pp. 8–24. See also Jenny Fleming and Rod Rhodes, 'Bureaucracy, Contracts and Networks: The Unholy Trinity and the Police', *Australian & New Zealand Journal of Criminology* (Vol. 38, No. 2, 2005), p. 195.

[16] Private communication, indigene, Kano, 2 December 2010.

cities such as Mogadishu than exhortations to trust, partnership and conventional forms of community policing.

A second obstacle to improved relations could be the SPF's position as the representative of a weak government that even now lacks legitimacy. Indeed, the SPF's legitimacy, in the eyes of the inhabitants of Mogadishu, is arguably stronger than that of the FGS, and its claim to have been established in 1948 or, depending on who is speaking, 1960 is generally accepted by not only Mogadishu's inhabitants, but also by the police forces of Somaliland and Puntland.[17] In contrast, the FGS exists only because the international community defends and supports it.

ICT's Ability to Connect People and Police

Trust, legitimacy and civilian accountability are widely considered to be key features of the style of community policing advocated by donors. Further, the export of the democratic policing models associated with it has become a major industry over the last two decades, with millions of dollars poured into ambitious projects intended to transfer 'professional' policing strategies, procedures and tactics to Africa's police.[18] Yet the results are unimpressive. Perhaps because of this, those advocates of reform are now looking to exploit the opportunities for change, transformation and innovation associated with ICT, even though ICT's record as a tool for improving people's quality of life, let alone their policing, is patchy; social realities are such that ICT cannot affect the overall incidence of insecurity, poverty and ill-health, least of all in societies such as Somalia's.[19] Further, much of the ICT used in police work is devoted to its technicalities and logistics (office equipment and records, for example, or forensic laboratories), rather than to the everyday needs of officers and communities, such as stationery, kettles and generators.[20] At the same time, sophisticated forms of ICT involving computers are prioritised over basic and inclusive forms such as the radio programmes and painted advertisements on which most people rely.

---

[17] See Alice Hills, 'Remembrance of Things Past: Somali Roads to Police Development', *Stability* (Vol. 3, No. 1, 2014).

[18] The best guide to democratic policing remains OECD DAC, *OECD DAC Handbook on Security System Reform: Supporting Security and Justice*.

[19] Chrisanthi Avergerou, 'Discourses on ICT and Development', *Information Technologies and International Development* (Vol. 6, No. 3, 2010); Ken Banks, 'Reflections on a Decade of Mobiles in Development', *Stability* (Vol. 2, No. 3, 2013).

[20] Contrast the Danish government's provision of office furniture, desktop computers, printers, folding chairs, tables, cabinets and, significantly, solar torches and solar lamps. *Shabelle News*, 'AU Police Hands Over Office Equipment to the Somali Police Force', 19 September 2017.

At first glance, the connection between ICT and police–community engagement in Africa is tenuous. The continent's police are notoriously corrupt, negligent and lacking in the political will, technical skills and resources needed for humane engagement practices. They are resistant to change, provide regime policing rather than community service, and are tolerated rather than trusted. General-duty constables in Mogadishu may have access to SIM cards or personal mobile phones but most are also untrained or illiterate and their pay is several months in arrears. With the exception of the occurrence books (ledgers for logging incidents and enquiries) at front desks, most police stations lack access to stationery and typewriters, let alone computers and internet connectivity.[21]

Knowledge about the potential connections between ICT and improved police–community engagement in Africa remains thin and heavily dependent on developments in Kenya, which is widely regarded as a beacon for the application of ICT to police-related issues. The desire to exploit ICT's potential for policing appears to be prompted primarily by the success in Kenya of ICT-based banking and open-source tracking systems such as: M-Pesa (a mobile phone-based money transfer and financing service), which was introduced in 2007; Ushahidi, which allows users to send crisis information via mobiles; and Usalama (Swahili for 'security'), a smartphone app that sends an emergency message to three predetermined contacts and is activated by shaking the phone three times while holding the volume button down, or tapping an emergency icon. In a further example of Kenya's embrace of ICT, the inspector general of the Kenya Police Service uses social media regularly, as do high-profile individuals such as Nakuru's 'Twitter chief'. The ease with which social media can be integrated into community policing enhances its appeal.[22] Somalia's cheap call tariffs and high rates of access to mobiles make the transfer of the Kenyan experience to Somalia seems plausible. More than half of the Somali population is thought to have access to mobile phones and affordable Chinese-made mobiles are widely available.[23] According to World Bank data, 51 out of every 100 adults have a mobile subscription, compared with 22 in 2013.[24]

There is much to be said for assuming that Kenya's experience can – and will – transfer. Somalis use mobile phones as a tool for sharing

---

[21] Author observations during visits to police stations in Hargeisa, Puntland's Garowe and Gardo, and Mogadishu, 2011–16.

[22] Duncan Omanga, '"Chieftaincy" in the Social Media Space: Community Policing in a Twitter Convened Baraza', *Stability* (Vol. 4, No. 1, 2015).

[23] *Quartz Africa*, 'More Phones, Few Banks and Years of Instability are Transforming Somalia to Cashless Society', 26 February 2016.

[24] *Ibid*.

information about family news, stock prices and animal health. Young people in Mogadishu have embraced social media as a way of connecting with the world, and apps such as Facebook are popular even among pastoralists; one told a Puntland journalist that Facebook allowed him to follow the latest events, keep in contact with friends and relatives abroad, and share good news: 'when two female camels gave birth, I snapped them and sent the photos to my brother'.[25] Above all, mobiles are used to transfer money, with around 40 per cent of adults using mobile money accounts such as M-Pesa.[26] Indeed, mobile money has replaced conventional cash and banking systems.

Despite the prevalence of mobile technology in Somalia, Kenya's approach has not been taken up enthusiastically. There is little evidence or cultural preference to suggest that mobiles are used for reporting crime and even less to suggest that the use of mobiles can help to lessen the distrust and poor response rates characterising everyday policing. Admittedly, many international researchers believe that connecting to social media changes people's expectations for real-time information, especially in relation to security,[27] but, while this may be true in Egypt, for example, there is as yet no evidence of social media affecting Somalia's security environment. With the exception of a few individuals, such as Lieutenant Colonel Zakia Hussein (the SPF's former director of community policing, who was educated in Sweden and the UK),[28] those charged with community safety have not fundamentally altered their ways of interacting with the public, and the SPF does not use social media to provide information or engage more directly with the population. Waberi's neighbourhood-watch scheme may use (offline) computers and photocopiers donated by the British Embassy, but its outreach and training activities rely on song and acting performances; for example, in July 2016 a community policing song was launched that was designed to persuade people that community safety is a shared responsibility.[29] Meanwhile, the Heegan Police Band is the SPF's most commonly used tool for public relations, appearing at, for example, football

---

[25] *Garowe Online*, 'Sitting Down with Somali Nomads', 26 June 2015.
[26] *Quartz Africa*, 'More Phones, Few Banks and Years of Instability are Transforming Somalia to Cashless Society'.
[27] Centre of African Studies, 'Social Media and Security', Edinburgh University, 2016, <http://www.cas.ed.ac.uk/research/grants_and_projects/sms_africa>, accessed 30 September 2016.
[28] Zakia Hussein, 2017, <https://twitter.com/zakiahussen?lang=en>, accessed 4 May 2017.
[29] See (and listen) at AMISOM, 'Somali Police Force Launches Community Policing Song', 17 July 2016, <http://amisom-au.org/2016/07/somali-police-force-launches-community-policing-song/>, accessed 18 July 2016.

matches and festivities.[30] Furthermore, observations by the author suggest that few police officers in Mogadishu – or Somaliland or Puntland – see any need to engage with the populace and, when they do, they rely on face-to-face contact, rather than ICT.[31]

ICT for Policing

Despite the limited extent of police–community engagement, intergovernmental organisations, donors and commercial companies regard ICT as a potential tool for improving reporting and resource allocation. Indeed, the belief that it can be transformational in areas from education and health to agriculture, competitiveness, financial services and, increasingly, public safety is evident from the expectations of the World Bank and the African Union.[32] Some telecommunications companies claim that public safety communications have been transformed in Africa by real-time data access, the migration to broadband data networks, the introduction of new tools and technologies as well as radios, smartphones and tablets, and by increased levels of community engagement and interaction.[33] Its reports claim that witnesses capture incidents using their mobile devices and share them on social media sites such as Facebook and Twitter, thereby creating a record of events that 'enforcement agencies' can use to prevent crime and resolve issues.

Crisis Hotlines

A more plausible form of ICT for policing and security-related purposes in Somalia is the crisis hotline. However, while Somalis from across the entities say that they want emergency response (and preferably toll-free)

---

[30] Hills, 'Is There Anybody There?'.
[31] Author's observations and conversations with mid-level and senior SPF officers in Nairobi and Mogadishu (September 2011, July 2016), Puntland officers in Garowe (September 2011), and Somaliland officers in Hargeisa (December 2015).
[32] eTransform Africa, 'Transformational Use of Information and Communication Technologies in Africa', World Bank, 2012, <http://web.worldbank.org/WBSITE/ EXTERNAL/TOPICS/EXTINFORMATIONANDCOMMUNICATIONANDTECHNOLO GIES/0,,contentMDK:23262578~pagePK:210058~piPK:210062~theSitePK:282823,00 .html>, accessed 30 September 2016; *This is Africa*, 'How Technology Can Transform Africa', 3 June 2015, <http://www.thisisafricaonline.com/News/How-technology-can-transform-Africa?ct=true>, accessed 30 September 2016.
[33] Motorola Solutions, 'Transforming Public Safety Communications in Europe and Africa: 4 Key Factors', 2016, p. 1, <https://www.motorolasolutions.com/en_xu/ communities/en/think-public-safety.entry.html/2016/06/17/transforming_public-h8un.html>, accessed 11 July 2016.

numbers, they rarely use them even when they are available. For example, AMISOM's 888 emergency response number, introduced in Mogadishu in late 2013,[34] should have helped to improve engagement and partnership because, like most such initiatives, it was intended to 'sensitize community resident's responsibilities towards reducing crime',[35] rather than prevent crime in isolation. AMISOM's police unit linked it to the implementation of a partnership with elders, women, youths and members of the business community, which was designed to strengthen security institutions, reduce insecurity and fight crime, as well as promote a zero-tolerance policy towards crime.[36] As usual in such cases, the AMISOM and SPF representatives present at the launch stressed the importance of the public sharing information with police officers to ensure the district's security. At a meeting in Karaan, for example, at which the deputy district commissioner urged residents to welcome community policing on the basis that they played a major role in keeping their neighbourhoods safe, secure and stable, the sweetener was that AMISOM had provided a toll-free line to connect the community to the police. This would, he said, encourage them to contact the authorities whenever they noticed anything suspicious.[37]

AMISOM had by then conducted similar meetings in Waberi, Hamar Weyne, Hamar Jajab and Shibis, where the projects had been received positively; local people were said to view the police differently as a result, and to be more willing to share intelligence and report crime. Certainly, the 888 emergency line was received enthusiastically by the chairwoman of Waberi District Women's Association. At a meeting with AMISOM's police unit earlier in the year, she promised to use the free number to work with security agencies to 'flush out' criminals: 'We have been waiting for this initiative ... which requires us to call a toll free number to report anything bad we see'.[38] In turn, a Ghanaian AMISOM officer stressed that with the support of Waberi's residents, 'we have been able to tell them how they can support the police in their own small way by way of giving information to the Somalia Police Force so that they can know

---

[34] *Horseed Media*, 'Shooting in Somalia? Dial 888 for Police', 2 December 2013.

[35] *Ibid.*

[36] AMISOM, 'AMISOM Community Policing Drive Extends to Karaan District', September 2015, <http://amisom-au.org/2015/09/amisom-community-policing-drive-extends-to-karaan-district/>, accessed 3 February 2016.

[37] *Ibid.*

[38] *Coastweek.com*, 'Somali Security Build Mogadishu Community Policing Partnerships', May 2015, <http://www.coastweek.com/3820-Somali-Police-and-AMISOM-build-community-policing-partnerships-in-Mogadishu.htm>, accessed 20 June 2016.

the criminals in their midst' and 'flush them' out.[39] But the number of calls actually received is minimal. In 2013, *Horseed Media* said that the 888 line received 40 calls per day from across Mogadishu's then sixteen districts,[40] but in July 2016, two senior AMISOM officers (both of whom had been in post for some months) said that they had only just heard of the initiative.[41] The line was still working in December 2016, when it received a few calls from business owners, but the general public was reported to be sceptical and did not trust the police, or more importantly, NISA, sufficiently to use it. As Egal reported in January 2017, 'people are afraid of the police, and there is a fear of retaliation if citizens complain and call the police'.[42]

This is not to suggest that ICT cannot increase engagement, rather that it is not enough to merely promote a number. This is evident when UNSOM's efforts to promote the Ceebla ('no shame') 5555 crisis line as a resource for gender-based violence are compared with those made by the Somali Women's Development Centre (SWDC) for their own crisis line.[43] Established originally in 2000, and with an increasingly polished website, the SWDC is an internationally supported but community-owned operation. Detailed statistics of the calls it receives are not available, but in conversations with the public relations manager of the centre it appeared that the two experienced volunteers running its crisis line receive a steady stream of calls from women subject to violence or abuse. More importantly, they respond in a practical and meaningful way by helping callers to navigate through the various services available, such as escorting them to clinics.[44]

In February 2017, the 5555 line's webpage included a section under 'Community Security' that talks about completing the first phase of a nine-month project, 'WCPU, Women Civilian Protection Unit', which is described as forming part of its peacebuilding and reconciliation project

---

[39] *Ibid.*; see also *AMISOM News*, 'Somali Police and AMISOM Police Build Community Policing Paternerships in Mogadishu', <http://amisom-au.org/2015/05/somali-police-and-amisom-police-build-community-policing-partnerships-in-mogadishu>/, accessed 26 January 2018.

[40] *Horseed Media*, 'Shooting in Somalia?'.

[41] Personal communication with senior AMISOM officers, July 2016.

[42] See Egal, 'Police Corruption, Radicalization and Terrorist Attacks in Mogadishu', p. 32.

[43] Responsibility – and credit – for the 5555 line was disputed in 2015 when SWDC's website repudiated links with UNSOM, although it now acknowledges international support. See Somali Women's Development Centre (SWDC) website, <http://www.swdcsom.org/ceebla-crisis-line-5555/>, accessed 4 March 2017; UNSOM, 'Somali IDPs Get Toll Free Line to Report Gender-Based Violence Cases', 3 November 2015.

[44] Author communications with SWDC officer, Mogadishu, 26 and 28 July 2016.

aimed at strengthening neighbourhood peace and security through community policing in five districts, including Waberi.[45] The first phase ran from December 2011 to May 2012, and the project was restarted in October 2012 and remains ongoing. SWDC claims to have registered 500 women representatives, with a Women Peace Vanguards Unit patrolling and reporting incidents to the SPF 'in order to restore basic rule of law at district level'.[46] It has not been possible to verify this, but the photographs of thirteen singers at the launch day show the importance of basic and inclusive forms of ICT in promoting such initiatives in societies with low literacy levels, and can be duplicated by photographs and videos of similar celebrations in Abdiaziz, Bonderre, Shingani and Waberi.[47] In other words, the use of ICT needs to be placed within the limits of its social, political and cultural context; the factors facilitating the translation of ICT into local practices need to identified, as do the circumstances leading to the adaptation of the new to the available, and the social spaces and timeframes in which these processes occur.

CCTV

Closed-circuit television (CCTV) is another form of ICT much favoured for crime prevention in the Global North, and is now in use in Mogadishu. In early March 2016, for example, the UN Support Office in Somalia sought tenders for the installation of UN-provided CCTV cameras in the city. A training course for users and operators was to be included in the tender, along with quarterly maintenance and incidental maintenance for twelve months.[48] By July 2016 there were approximately 40 cameras in operation, monitoring traffic and security at high-profile buildings such as regional police headquarters and the Bank of Somalia, although there was no monitoring room.

This changed in January 2017 when the UNDP's Rule of Law project for CCTV was formally inaugurated and noted that installing CCTV cameras across key locations supported the Ministry of Internal Security because it meant that the SPF 'are able to monitor high risk areas and help law enforcement investigate and solve crime by using CCTV as

---

[45] SWDC, 'Peace Building & Reconciliation', <http://www.swdcsom.org/peace-building-reconciliation/>, accessed 4 March 2017.
[46] SWDC, 'Community Security', <http://www.swdcsom.org/what-we-do/community-security/>, accessed 4 March 2017.
[47] *Ibid.*
[48] 12b, 'Tenders | Installation of UN Provided CCTV Cameras in Mogadishu … ', 2016, <https://www.tendersontime.com/tenders/africa/kenya/installation-of-un-provided-cctv-cameras-in-mogadishu-somalia-to-include-53acf7/>, accessed 4 March 2017.

evidence', as well as facilitating the SPF's rapid response to security threats.[49] The project trained fifteen officers on how to operate the CCTV system, provided security during its installation, refurbished the CCTV control room at the SPF headquarters, and provided a generator using the Ministry of Finance's procurement system. As the SPF's deputy commissioner, General Bashir Abdi Mohamed, proudly announced, '[t]his is a big step forward for the Somali Police in preventing and prosecuting crime in the capital. We are hoping to increase the cameras thereby increasing peace in Mogadishu city'.[50]

Nevertheless, CCTV's primary target is terrorism and its associated forms of crime. And there is good reason for this, with the most high-profile prompt being footage from the airport showing the moment on 2 February 2016 when a man in a security jacket handed a laptop containing a bomb to a suicide bomber, who detonated the device on a Daallo Airlines flight as it left Mogadishu for Djibouti.[51] Another example occurred in June 2016 when, during Ramadan (when insecurity typically increases), Waberi's district police commissioner used an appeal to crime prevention to justify a pilot project based on CCTV cameras along a major road through the district. He said that the first batch of cameras, which had been installed around the district police station area along Makka Al-Mukarrama road, would 'enable the law enforcement agencies to verify identities of those involved in latent criminal activities, while closely monitoring the city'.[52] He then asked the public to help the police protect the city by reporting any suspicious sightings in their neighbourhood. Seven months later, CCTV recordings of a bombing on Lido Beach became available at Africa.liveuamap.com,[53] while February 2017's elections produced reports of hidden cameras on the main roads leading into the central area.[54] But whether CCTV provides more than graphic images in the aftermath of incidents is open to question because cameras

---

[49] Somalia UN MPTF 1 Rev. 6, 'Programme Annual Progress Report. Period: Quarter 1 2017', pp. 2, 15, 30.
[50] *Ibid.*
[51] Gianluca Mezzofiore, 'How Terrorist Was Handed a Bomb AFTER Clearing Customs: Chilling Mogadishu Airport CCTV Shows Moment Somali Jet Bomber was Passed a Laptop Containing Hidden Explosives', *MailOnline*, 7 February 2016.
[52] Mogadishu Centre for Research & Studies (MCRS), 'Mogadishu Police to Install Surveillance Cameras in Key City Places', 14 June 2016, <http://mogadishucenter. com/English/2016/06/14/mogadishu-police-to-install-surveillance-cameras-in-key-city-places/>, accessed 21 June 2016.
[53] *AfricaLive*, 'Mogadishu: This is the CCTV Record of Today's Explosion from Lido Beach', January 2017, <http://africa.liveuamap.com/en/2017/2-january-mogadishu-this-is-the-cctv-record-of-todays-explosion>, accessed 9 February 2017.
[54] Mohamed Jeelle, 'Somalia: Hidden Cameras were Fixed on the Main Roads in Mogadishu for the First Time', Mareeg.com, 5 February 2017.

along Makka Al-Mukarrama road did not prevent a car bomb destroying the police station on 30 July 2017.[55]

Basic and Inclusive ICT

CCTV cameras are too vulnerable to be much more than a gesture in a city such as Mogadishu, and their usefulness is limited by the challenges of coordinating, consolidating and implementing the results. Additional obstacles in the way of ICT (and mobiles in particular) being used for crime-reporting and policing-related purposes include weak central government, tight links between businessmen and politicians, widespread suspicion of NISA, the existence of a strong private telecommunications sector that in the absence of regulation has been able to develop influential political and commercial networks, low literacy rates, poverty and high rates of theft.[56] Hence, perhaps, the preference even of literate residents for using the most basic and inclusive forms of ICT in community-oriented engagement.

Consequently, in cities such as Mogadishu, the most appropriate tools for improving police–community engagement will have broad reach and relatively low costs. They will be easily used, rely on existing infrastructure, use common data formats and extend accessible systems and services to hard-to-reach populations. Examples of such technologies include SMS, radio, voice telephony, blackboards, megaphones and, importantly for Somali society, cartoons, murals and theatrical performances, which can provide the training, guidance and encouragement necessary for improving crime-reporting (although probably not police response rates). As Chapter III's account of Waberi's experience shows, donated computers can act as attractive recording or collating devices, but information is best collected in person or by word of mouth, and the most appropriate ways to do this are taught using cartoons, posters and theatre. In this way, as far as Somali society is concerned, ICT is better understood as 'images, cartoons and theatre'.

Comparing Experience

The picture presented here raises important questions about police–community engagement in environments characterised by high access to

---

[55] Hussein Mohamed and Mohamed Ibrahim, 'Car Bomb Kills at Least 6 and Injures 13 Others in Mogadishu', *New York Times,* 30 July 2017.

[56] See De Waal, *The Real Politics of the Horn of Africa*, pp. 115–16, 119–23. In January 2018, the FGS announced that it will create an independent regulatory agency for telecommunications. See Balancing Act, 'Somalia Takes Steps towards Establishing Regulator', 26 January 2018, <https://www.balancingact-africa.com/news/telecoms-en/42549/somalia-takes-steps-towards-establishing-regulator>, accessed 30 January 2018.

mobiles but low literacy levels and minimal police response rates. Mogadishu's dangerous environment provides one answer, but the question then arises as to how its experience compares to that of safer cities, such as Hargeisa, capital of Somaliland, but once part of former Somalia.

More importantly, Mogadishu's experience raises questions about the everyday choices of its inhabitants in shaping low-level police–community engagement. The discussion in the next chapter uses public responses to a text alert project in Hargeisa to explore these issues. In focusing on how local expectations are actually fulfilled, rather than how donors think they should be, there is little evidence to suggest that access to ICT leads to more responsive or accountable policing. This confirms the hypothesis that what the police do is shaped as much by community expectations as by the technologies available. From this perspective, the key to understanding police–community engagement is to be found in the knowledge, skills and resources police need to fulfil local societal, rather than international, expectations.

V. HARGEISA'S MODEST EXPERIMENT

Police–community engagement in Mogadishu's districts varies according to clan dynamics, personalities and security issues. Expectations are low on both sides, but the physical vulnerability of police officers and their stations means that some form of working relationship must be developed; it may be based on avoidance or acquiescence, rather than trust, but it must represent a locally acceptable form of engagement.[1]

This suggests that the key to understanding police–community engagement is in the knowledge, skills and resources police need to fulfil local, rather than international, expectations regarding the management of low-level security. This interpretation helps to move the debate about police–community relations forward from the now standard assertion that public trust is the key variable influencing police effectiveness and the legitimacy of police actions.[2] Contrary to Boateng, collaborative relationships do not depend on institutional legitimacy, trust or procedural justice.[3] Rather, it depends on a range of context-specific variables.

Mogadishu's environment is unique, so its experience of mobiles providing a two-way technology capable of reaching low-income or marginalised populations and affecting their response to crime does not necessarily transfer to more remote Somali cities, such as Baidoa and Kismayo (140 and 250 miles by air to the west and south respectively). Nevertheless, Mogadishu's experience raises general questions about the

---

[1] This chapter draws on Alice Hills, 'Is There Anybody There? Police, Communities and Communications Technology in Hargeisa', *Stability* (Vol. 6, No. 1, 2017), pp. 1–16.
[2] Mike Hough et al., 'Procedural Justice, Trust, and Institutional Legitimacy', *Policing* (Vol. 4, 2010), pp. 203–10; Francis Boateng, 'Police Legitimacy in Africa: a Multilevel Multinational Analysis', Policing & Society (20 January 2017), doi:10.1080/10439463. 2017.1280034.
[3] The re-emergence or restructuring of Somalia's police forces since 2012 is not dependent on institutional structures or institutional memory either. See Alice Hills, 'Remembrance of Things Past: Somali Roads to Police Development', *Stability* (Vol. 3, No. 1, 2014), p. 11.

connection between technology and police–community relations in fragile Southern cities: can ICT help to facilitate trust and communication between police and residents in societies with low literacy rates but high access to mobiles? What aspects of ICT help residents to manage their everyday security? Is one-to-one communication between police and residents as important as community-based engagement? How important is the police station as a site for engagement? When is ICT used creatively or in an innovative fashion? What is the role of initiative in police–community interactions? We know what affects policing in Mogadishu's dangerous districts, but what shapes low-level policing in less fragile urban environments?

We can begin to answer these questions and explore the possibilities for generalising from Mogadishu's experience by looking at the results of a text alert system introduced into New Hargeisa, a relatively safe district in Somaliland's capital, Hargeisa. Doing so also allows us to address the connection between ICT and police–community engagement in environments characterised by high access to mobile telephones but minimal police-response rates, and these are found across sub-Saharan Africa. More importantly, using residents' responses to the text alert project enables the exploration of the everyday choices shaping low-level police–community engagement. It shows how local expectations are, rather than should be, fulfilled. This goes some way towards rebalancing a picture otherwise skewed towards the agenda and expectations of international organisations such as the EU and the UN.

Macalin Haaruun's Text Alert Experiment

On 19 August 2015, the Somaliland Ministry of Interior launched a text alert community–police engagement programme at a small police station in the Macalin Haaruun district of New Hargeisa.[4] Promoted enthusiastically by the minister and developed by advisers from EUCAP Nestor,[5] a civilian mission forming part of the EU's external action programme, the project's objective was straightforward: members of the public would use their mobile phones to alert the police by text to security issues requiring attention. In becoming 'the eyes and ears' of the police, residents would help to improve police–community engagement and local security.

---

[4] This chapter is based on a visit to Hargeisa in December 2015, and is informed by author discussions with EUCAP and Somaliland officials and officers, between 2014 and 2017. It also draws on Hills, 'Is There Anybody There?'.
[5] EUCAP Nestor (the EU Maritime Capacity Building Mission to Somalia) was renamed EUCAP Somalia (the EU Capacity Building Mission in Somalia) on 1 March 2017.

But the project did not work out as EUCAP Nestor hoped. In the days that followed the launch, the publicity campaign evaporated, the minister returned to his office, the station's commander went on leave for six weeks, the mobiles donated to the police stayed in their boxes, and the station's radio room was locked. By December 2015, few if any calls had been received.

Why should a modest and unsuccessful experiment in a dusty residential district in a comparatively stable but internationally unrecognised republic deserve attention in a discussion focusing on security and police–community relations in Mogadishu? The situation in Somaliland is in many respects different from that in Mogadishu – the Somaliland Police Force (SLPF) is the most developed of the three main Somali forces, and crime and political discontent are relatively low. Hargeisa is not as secure as it was in 2015 or 2016, and its security record has been undermined by a combination of issues, including: financial crisis; drought; the increasing presence of radical Islamism; and the impact of regional machinations.[6] Kidnappings and street robberies involving knife-wielding youths have increased, as has glue-sniffing and fighting among homeless children and youths displaced from rural areas. Social dislocation is exacerbated by the presence of IDPs and the economic migrants who make up 56% of the population living in the city's settlements and neighbourhoods.[7] However, few expect the police to respond to incidents.

As in Mogadishu, Hargeisa's inhabitants rely on clan affiliation for protection, and most look first to clan elders (traditional justice systems) for justice in all but the more violent crimes; only migrants and IDPs lacking clan protection use formal justice procedures.[8] The views of Hargeisa's inhabitants on the SLPF deserve attention because the city's environment allows for the collection of detail that supplements those

---

[6] *Indian Ocean Newsletter*, 'How an Oasis of Stability Became a Powder Keg', 10 February 2017; *Indian Ocean Newsletter*, 'A Convoluted Succession', 8 September 2017; OilPrice.com, 'Geopolitical Time Bomb: Chaos in Somaliland Could Trigger Regional Conflict', 1 March 2017, <http://oilprice.com/Geopolitics/Africa/Geopolitical-Time-Bomb-Chaos-In-Somaliland-Could-Trigger-Regional-Conflict.html>, accessed 25 March 2017; Abdillahi Hussein, 'The Rising Cost of Living in Somaliland: A Threat to Peace and Social Stability', *Hiiraan Online*, 18 May 2017; see also Critical Threats, 'The Gulf Contest for the Horn of Africa', 26 September 2017, <https://www.criticalthreats.org/analysis/the-gulf-contest-for-the-horn-of-africa>, accessed 27 September 2017.
[7] *AMISOM Daily Media Monitoring*, 'Homeless Children Sniff Glue to Take "Away the Pain" of Surviving Somalia's Streets', 6 September 2017.
[8] UNHCR, 'Internal Displacement Profiling in Hargeisa', 2015, p. 32, <http://reliefweb.int/sites/reliefweb.int/files/resources/original_Hargeisa_Report_Web.pdf>, accessed 4 March 2017.

available in Waberi'. The experiment offers contextualised insights into both the specifics of police–community engagement in a relatively controlled urban environment and the use of mobiles as a two-way technology capable of reaching low-income or marginalised populations.

Hargeisa's record is regionally unexceptional as far as police–community relations are concerned, and so too is its failure to adopt ICT-based crisis lines. As with Mogadishu's 888 emergency reporting line, the two landline emergency hotline numbers introduced in 2013 by the Somaliland's police commissioner, Abdillahi Fadal Iman, received few if any calls. There is no equivalent to the 5555 reporting hotline, but even if there were it would likely be unsuccessful; the record of reporting lines elsewhere in Africa suggests that 5555's success is atypical. Indeed, the fate of most such lines suggests that the failure of ICT (and text-based systems in particular) for crime prevention is only to be expected. Overall, the experiment at Macalin Haruun cautions against overly ambitious discussions of international donor-oriented police–community engagement.

Rationale for a Text Alert System
Launched by the Ministry of Interior, although originally identified and developed by two Hargeisa-based EUCAP police advisers, the text alert project was a way to prevent crime, target resources and thereby improve police–community engagement in New Hargeisa. Drawing on their personal experience of a text alert system used in rural areas of the Republic of Ireland, the advisers developed a plan for blending crime-reporting and community engagement using text alerts as a tool for diffusing knowledge. The aim was to enhance local security while helping the Somaliland police to target scarce resources in the areas where they were most needed.[9]

The police station of Macalin Haruun was chosen by the ministry on the basis that it was small and easily monitored, and its English-speaking commander would facilitate communication with EUCAP. It was also a showpiece, having been opened by the UN Development Programme (UNDP) as a model station in 2012.[10] In other words, it was a place where police and community were expected to interact.[11] In the event, the

---

[9] European Union External Action, 'PR 31_2015: Text Alert Community Police Engagement Programme Launched in Somaliland', 19 August 2015, <https://www.eucap-nestor.eu/en/press_office/news/1306/>, accessed 24 August 2015.
[10] UNDP, 'Somaliland Opens First "Model Police Station"', 2012, <http://www.so.undp.org/content/somalia/en/home/ourwork/crisispreventionandrecovery/successstories/Somaliland.html>, accessed 2 March 2015.
[11] See also Cynthia Lum and Nicholas Fyfe, 'Space, Place, and Policing: Exploring Geographies of Research and Practice', *Policing* (Vol. 9, No. 3, 2015).

project quickly lost momentum. At the time of the author's visit on 9 December 2015, signs in Somali and English indicated the offices allocated to, for instance, the commander and the women and children's desk, but the compound was cluttered, the radio room from which the system is administered was locked, the most IT-proficient officer (a woman) had been replaced by a less competent man, and the front desk's occurrence book was not up-to-date.

With the benefit of hindsight, it is evident that the project's chances of success were slim: the text-based system was introduced into an oral culture in which a high percentage of the population is illiterate (there are no examples of successful call-based or text-based crime-prevention lines operating in the region), and neither the Ministry nor EUCAP was fully committed to the continuation of the project, which was, moreover, run on a shoestring budget of €8,500.

It is difficult to avoid the conclusion that the project says more about donor dynamics and well-intentioned advisers than the state of police–community engagement in Hargeisa. Yet the initial assumptions of EUCAP's advisers were not unrealistic. Somaliland has high rates of access to mobiles and low tariffs, its government actively promotes ICT-based solutions for the management of criminal records, and anecdotal accounts of people's willingness to 'tell the government' – that is, ring the police – about crime-related issues suggests that police–community communications were relatively good.

Although there are no open-source analyses of police–community relations in Hargeisa, a combination of NGO surveys and informal responses from residents living near Macalin Haaruun station suggest additional reasons as to why EUCAP considered the project plausible. For example, reports of officers demanding payment for responding to crimes and of stations being used as detention centres were offset by anecdotal evidence of residents being treated politely.[12] Furthermore, although Hargeisa's OCVP has yet to survey security perceptions in the city, surveys conducted elsewhere in Somaliland indicate surprisingly positive attitudes towards police, with those from towns such as Buroa, 178 km to the east of Hargeisa, suggestive of what might be found.[13] Buroa's

---

[12] Human Rights Centre, 'Human Rights Centre: Annual Review 2015', 2015, <http://www.hrcsomaliland.org/attachments/article/154/Official%20Annual%20Review%202015.pdf>, accessed 17 December 2015.

[13] OCVP, 'Buroa: District Conflict and Security Assessment', 2015, pp. xii, 26, <http://ocvp.org/docs/2015/Wave4/Burao%20-%20DCSA%20Report%20-%202015.pdf>, accessed 26 January 2018; see also OCVP, 'Borama: District Conflict and Security Assessment', 2015, pp. 6–9, <http://ocvp.org/docs/2015/Wave7/Borama%20DCSA%202015.pdf>, accessed 9 November 2016.

respondents say that the police are their main security provider, supplemented by the activities of informal groups such as security committees and night guards.[14] Almost all respondents are aware of the location of the town's police stations and the time it takes to walk to them (OCVP uses this as an indicator of people's awareness of state provision), and almost all say that they prefer to report civil disputes and petty and serious crime to the police rather than to elders.

Importantly, respondents also stress that communities should support their under-resourced police by taking responsibility for their own security and by giving information to the police,[15] thus confirming trends in community policing seen in countries such as Ethiopia and Nigeria. When combined with widespread access to mobile phones and, critically, EUCAP's need to be seen to act, it is unsurprising that EUCAP's advisers were encouraged to believe that a text alert system could be introduced successfully.

Model Police Stations

One of the strategies donors use to change police–community relations in cities such as Hargeisa and Mogadishu involves the creation of model police stations. This requires building or renovating a police station according to international design principles and operating procedures. Such stations emphasise service provision, which requires designated places for public access, weapons' storage, a women and children's desk, and separate male and female cells and lavatories. They do not address ICT, but in practice residents rarely share donors' enthusiasm for ICT, let alone the gender equality, empowerment and protection for the vulnerable promoted in the name of such stations. These inappropriate, donor-driven goals, combined with budgetary, organisational and political constraints, mean that the expense of such stations is too high to be sustainable, let alone replicable across the country concerned.[16]

This was the fate of the model station opened by the UNDP in Macalin Haaruun in 2012. Designed to strengthen community participation in policing and 'foster partnership' via community contact groups involving elders, women, youths, NGOs, and businesses, its 70 officers were deployed to 'provide security services for 30,000 people in local communities'.[17] Officers were to collaborate with communities to identify

---

[14] *Ibid.*
[15] OCVP, 'Buroa', p. 23.
[16] Independent Commission for Aid Impact (ICAI), 'Review of UK Development Assistance for Security and Justice', 2015, p. 26.
[17] UNDP, 'Somaliland Opens Model Station'.

insecurity, while communities were to support officers in responding to insecurity. In the event, the project was never rolled out across Hargeisa and there is no evidence that it achieved its goals.

Mobile Phone Use

Although there were no significant developments in police–community relations in the three years that followed the text alert experiment, access to mobile phones increased dramatically, and by 2015 mobiles had had a marked impact on, for example, money transfers and communications between Hargeisa and the Somaliland diaspora in the US, Scandinavia and EU member states. Its failure to affect police provision and street-level security is consequently notable, especially when data from the World Bank and Gallup cite mobile phone ownership in Somaliland at 70 per cent, on a par with Kenya and well above the regional median.[18] In practice, access is even higher because mobiles are often shared and it is possible to subscribe to mobile services without buying a phone; many people buy a pre-paid SIM card which they use in other people's mobiles.[19] Tariffs in Somaliland's unregulated industry are also among the lowest in Africa.[20] More significantly, the money transfer and telecommunications industries have used ICT to bridge the country's governance gap, exploiting mobiles to leapfrog the limited number of landlines, banks and roads, and there is no obvious technological reason why ICT could not help to mitigate Hargeisa's poor-quality police response.[21] There are, however, functional and cultural reasons. Whether police or residents bear the primary responsibility for shaping the resultant style of police–community relations is debatable,

---

[18] World Bank, 'Information and Communication Technologies', 2016, <http://www.worldbank.org/en/topic/ict/overview#1>, accessed 28 April 2017; see also Gallup, 'Disparities in Cellphone Ownership Pose Challenges in Africa', 17 February 2016, <http://www.gallup.com/poll/189269/disparities-cellphone-ownership-pose-challenges-africa.aspx>, accessed 28 April 2017.

[19] Jeffrey James and Mila Versteeg, 'Mobile Phones in Africa: How Much Do We Really Know?', *Social Indicators Research* (Vol. 84, No. 1, 2007), pp. 117–26; Lishan Adam, 'Ethiopia ICT Sector Performance Review 2009/2010', ResearchnetICT, <http://www.researchictafrica.net/publications/Policy_Paper_Series_Towards_Evidence-based_ICT_Policy_and_Regulation_-_Volume_2/Vol%202%20Paper%209%20-%20Ethiopia%20ICT%20Sector%20Performance%20Review%202010.pdf>, accessed 13 September 2015.

[20] *Budde.com.au*, 'Somalia - Telecoms, Mobile and Broadband - Statistics and Analyses', 2015, <http://www.budde.com.au/Research/Somalia-Telecoms-Mobile-and-Broadband-Statistics-and-Analyses.html>, accessed 13 September 2015.

[21] See Alice Hills, 'Off-Road Policing: Communications Technology and Government Authority in Somaliland', *International Affairs* (Vol. 92, No. 5, 2016).

although officers' role as representatives of the state and government suggests that their attitudes are key.

Somaliland Police Force

Regardless of technological issues, the SLPF has a chequered history, although it is more positive than the SPF's. The combination of a predominantly Isaaq population (one of the main Somali clans) with the country's resilient customary law, active civil society, relatively peaceful capital and orderly presidential elections have helped to ensure that Somaliland has the most developed police system in the former Somalia. The number of officers based in Hargeisa is unknown, although there are approximately 6,800 officers throughout Somaliland,[22] and their current rank structure and occupational culture are more civilianised than the SPF. Although a significant number are unfit or illiterate, most have received a basic introduction to rights-based policing and the Somaliland police charter and constitution. As in Mogadishu's police, the more educated are aware of international practices and procedures even as they filter them through local interests and dispositions.

Increasingly, Somaliland's police force must also accommodate people's familiarity with, and use of, ICT. Many officers in Hargeisa have little or no interest in ICT, but it is clear from personal conversations with senior officers and recent recruits in December 2015 (most notably in the Immigration Police, which does not, however, deal directly with the public) that some embrace ICT as a tool for addressing issues ranging from street crime to uncontrolled migration, Al-Shabaab, Daesh and the conflict in Yemen.[23] Nonetheless, there is no evidence to suggest that ICT can address the Somaliland police's more immediate challenge of inadequate resources and personnel shortages, both of which impact on the low-ranking general-duty officers working in districts such as New Hargeisa.

Whether police–community engagement is unsatisfactory as far as such officers are concerned is, however, debatable. On the one hand, internal displacement from drought-affected areas has exacerbated the fragmentation of clan cohesiveness formerly found in Hargeisa, so police work is less predictable, and the notion of community may mean less. Yet the absence of a significant change in officers' approaches to people living near Macalin Haaruun police station – and vice versa – over the last two or three years suggests that the situation is in some way tolerable to both sides. Donors may argue that officers' jobs are safer and easier when

---

[22] Hills, 'Somalia Works', p. 97.
[23] Author interviews with senior police officers, Hargeisa, 11 December 2015.

they work in partnership with local people, identifying and solving problems collaboratively and responding to incidents quickly and efficiently, but in practice most officers, in Hargeisa as in Mogadishu, spend their day in their station compounds because there is no culture of response by the police, let alone of partnership with or service to inhabitants. Access to ICT is highly unlikely to change this.

The SLPF has had no history of engaging with the public since the 1960s and is not yet fully civilianised; there is no culture of recording or reporting ordinary crime, and while the 2012 Police Reform Bill is still on the statute book, there is no evidence of police – or politicians or residents – looking for fundamental change. The retention of good recruits may be a problem in many parts of Somaliland's law enforcement system, but this reportedly has more to do with youths' unwillingness to undertake basic training courses and take orders than discontent with the system as such.[24]

Low-ranking officers seem relatively content with the status quo; their job may be of low status, but they have free clothes (uniforms) and while they may not get paid much – or regularly – neither do they need to work hard or protect their job against political interference in the way that senior officers do. The picture emerging suggests that police behaviour conforms to local expectations and requirements, and that ICT plays no part in this. Nevertheless, the reasons why the text alert experiment failed help to throw light on both the nature of police–community relations and everyday security provision in a relatively safe environment and the commonalities New Hargeisa shares with Waberi.

Why the Text Alert Experiment Failed

The potential success of Macalin Haaruun's text alert experiment depended on two elements: the willingness of the public to contact officers via mobile messages; and officers' willingness to answer the call, log it, verify it as legitimate and, critically, respond by deploying to the scene. Officers also needed the ability and motivation to cascade alerts.

The text alert system was a simple, robust system that should easily have handled several thousand messages. The station was open 24/7, and taking messages should not have been a problem because eight men and eight women officers had been trained, with eight (half male and half female) covering three shifts. The system was basic but reliable, which was important when only 1–2 per cent of the population in Somaliland was thought to have access to a SIM card or mobile. It was built on a SIM

---

[24] Author interview with international adviser, Hargeisa, 7 December 2015.

box with cards that were connected to a laptop computer that created groups and sent messages. Actions were logged on police mobiles and in a log book, keyed into the system manually, and a message was sent over the computer system. In theory this should have taken about 30 seconds, but the process was actually haphazard, illustrating the obstacles in the way of exploiting ICT.

The officer taking the message needed to take full details of the complaint or information before a more senior officer could decide on its seriousness and the appropriate response. Unfortunately, not all officers have the necessary keyboard skills, senior officers are not always available and information is lost if the phone is mislaid. Issues of confidentiality are a potential concern for the ministry and EUCAP, as is data protection and the ways in which information is to be used in the courts. Also, the information received is sometimes linked directly to interventions, but this does not happen systematically. It did not, for example, prompt police to break up a fight at a graveyard on the outskirts of Hargeisa early on 8 December 2015, even though a neighbour had rung to warn the police that trouble was imminent.[25]

Explanations for the text alert system's failure include the unwillingness of President Ahmed Mohamed Mohamoud's (Silanyo) government to encourage community engagement as well as the failure on the part of the Somaliland authorities and EUCAP to provide the resources and commitment needed for its success and sustainability. The practical reasons for people not using text alerts include the lack of an emergency number (the Ministry of Interior reserves 100 for crises) and the complications created by the independence of Somaliland's main telecoms providers, Telesom, Somtel and NationLink;[26] some mobiles are accessed by three or four SIM cards, while even the abortive 2013 landline emergency hotline had to provide numbers for both Telesom and Somtel, none of which were short or memorable (Telesom's numbers were 520172 and 520257, while Somtel's were 7923169 and 7923170). Like Mogadishu's 888 reporting line, the two landline emergency hotline numbers introduced by the SLP's commissioner Brigadier General Abdillahi Fadal Iman in 2013 received few if any calls.[27] The cost of messages is also a factor in its failure. Officers do not pay for responding

---

[25] Author interview with senior officers, Hargeisa, 8 December 2016.

[26] See Budde.com, 'Somalia - Telecoms, Mobile and Broadband - Statistics and Analyses', 2017, <https://www.budde.com.au/Research/Somalia-Telecoms-Mobile-and-Broadband-Statistics-and-Analyses>, accessed 2 February 2018.

[27] Somalilandsun, 'Police Issue Emergency Hotline Numbers' 17 May 2013, <http://www.somalilandsun.com/2013/05/17/somaliland-police-issue-emergency-hotline-numbers/>, accessed 3 September 2015.

to or verifying a call, but the public must, and the SIM card used must be prepaid and in credit. The text alert system is an element within a broad approach to police–community engagement and can be described as community policing but, as in Mogadishu, such policing reminds many Somalilanders of the military monitoring and control methods used in the 1970s and 1980s.

In addition to the fundamental reasons outlined above for the failure of the text alert system and, more importantly, the low take-up of ICT for communicating with the police, the failure of the experiment may be a blend of local realities and cultural preferences. Speed of response is the main criterion by which policing provision is judged, but officers do not respond rapidly in central Hargeisa during the day, let alone on the outskirts at night, so people rely instead on informal, area-based security arrangements: in other words community policing or neighbourhood-watch schemes. Each district pays its community group a small sum of money each month to safeguard its area at night, and such groups respond more quickly than the police. One reason for this is that the groups are integral parts of their communities in a way that officers are not; the youths, women and elders involved in the groups are known throughout the districts in which they operate, and people trust them. However, not everyone is enthusiastic. Some residents argue that 'guard men' minimise theft and are sometimes able to return stolen items, but others say that community groups do not provide better security because they are rag-tag groups without formal offices or contact points, which makes them inaccessible. Also, the groups' members would like to use mobiles to cascade verbal alerts – although not texts – but in practice most cannot afford to pay for mobiles and theft is a common problem. They cannot afford to pay for transport either. Meanwhile, many fear that the groups are managed by the government for its own purpose or infiltrated by Al-Shabaab or ex-criminals. There are clearly problems associated with this form of policing but for most it has to be an acceptable solution.

What Local People Really Think

The text alert system failed to achieve its objective of receiving and cascading information because local people did not use it. The reasons for this have yet to receive systematic attention from EUCAP and the Ministry of Interior, but a partial explanation can be deduced from focus groups carried out with a demographically and socially representative range of residents from Macalin Haaruun and five neighbouring districts in March 2016.[28]

Each member of a team of ten Somali researchers from Transparency Solutions, a Hargeisa-based development consultancy, conducted eighteen interviews over the course of a week, with two or three interviews completed each day. Some of the researchers came from the local area, which gave them easy access to potential participants, while the inclusion of men and women meant that the team was able to reach a demographically representative selection of residents. Drawing on their experience of working in Hargeisa, the team organised discussions with 180 adult volunteers from six districts around Macalin Haaruun station. Fifty were interviewed in Macalin Haaruun, 28 in Mahmid Haibe, 28 in Ahmed Dhagah (a separate enclave that became anti-government in the aftermath of shootings in 2012), 28 in 26-June (a district on the other side of the main road to Macalin Haaruun), 25 in Ibraahim Koodbuur (a district containing a well-known IDP camp), and 21 in Ga'an Libah. Of the 180 respondents, 96 (53.3 per cent) were male and 84 (46.6 per cent) female. Eighty-two (45.5 per cent) were married, 81 (45 per cent) single, eight (4.4 per cent) divorced and seven (3.8 per cent) widowed; the status of the remaining respondents was unknown. Twenty-nine (16.1 per cent) were educated at madrassa, thirteen (7.2 per cent) were educated to primary school level, 25 (14 per cent) to intermediate level, and 43 (24 per cent) attended secondary school, while 31 (17.2 per cent) were educated at tertiary level and eleven (6.1 per cent) were self-schooled. Twenty-three (12.7 per cent) were illiterate.

Respondents were asked if they had contacted the police and, if so, where, when and why. Those who had were asked whether they had used mobiles, how they had been treated, and whether they would contact the police in future. Ninety said that they had contacted the police in the year before the text alert system was introduced and 25 in the period since. But it is not clear why they contacted the police because 160 said that they did not report a crime. Although 140 said that the police treated them politely (25 said they did not), 174 said that they would go back to the police, with nine answering 'maybe'.

Asked how people normally communicate with the police, 158 said that the youths, women, elders and businessmen involved in community-based groups visit their local station, which is the recognised – and seemingly preferred – site for engagement. They, like the Nigerians and South Africans that Cooper-Knock and Owen met,[29] prefer to speak to officers face to face because only then can they develop or reinforce the personal relationship needed for an officer to respond. Significantly, 35 said that they had rung their local station using a mobile but the police had failed to respond to their calls. No-one had used the text alert system.

---

[28] Based on focus groups conducted on the author's behalf by Amel Saeed and Mohammed Yusuf, Transparency Solutions.

[29] Cooper-Knock and Owen, 'Between Vigilantism and Bureaucracy'.

Respondents appeared surprisingly tolerant of the gap between what is possible and what actually happens. When asked how the use of mobile phones might improve security, 167 said mobiles allowed information to be spread quickly and police to call for back-up from units further away from the station. But none referred to ICT unprompted and ICT evidently plays no part in their experience or their ideal model of policing. Public awareness of the police's inadequate resources and flaws was explored by asking respondents how they would like to see the SLPF develop and what kind of police they would like their children to encounter. Half (91) thought in terms of resources, stating that police should get more financial support, equipment and stations; 45 argued in favour of an improvement in officers' status in the community, while 56 hoped to see police reach the standards in developed countries. Respondents in Macalin Haaruun said police would respond to crime more quickly and effectively if they received more equipment (21), a salary increase (thirteen), education (five), followed the law properly (three), received better treatment within the police (two), and stopped chewing khat (two). But no-one mentioned toll-free lines for text alerts, crime prevention or rape, although 28 stressed the desirability of a direct contact line for emergencies and improved communications more generally. The ideal for all respondents, and what they hoped their children would encounter, is honest police who perform their tasks quickly and do not harm civilians.

The building bricks of police–community relations were addressed using questions about police work and whether other groups provide security more quickly. All respondents agreed that the police's job includes securing peace and stability, from the village to national level, and providing a quick response when insecurity threatens. Significantly, 150 respondents said that local people should help the police to do their jobs more effectively, although none explained how this might be achieved. But an idea of what the police's purpose is thought to involve is evident from the explanations given by a group of eighteen respondents from across the six districts. Nine described the police as a tool for punishing criminals and 'the guilty', five emphasised the police's responsibility for ensuring rights and property, while two said the police exists solely to hurt, arrest and restrain people. Two said that they were not aware of what the police do.

Perhaps the most surprising result came in response to questions about the text alert experiment. When questioned, only five of the 142 respondents had heard of it, even though 47 (38 per cent) had friends or relatives in the police and 74 (51 per cent) had been to Macalin Haaruun station. The reasons for this are unclear but probably owe much to the filtering effects of cultural or social preference. People with access to mobiles or SIM cards are comfortable ringing the police, especially when they have been the victim of robbers or wish to 'tell the government' about a potential incident, but they do not use text messaging. This may reflect literacy levels or Somaliland's oral or political culture, or it may be no more than an acknowledgement of the police's inability to respond quickly.

In this way, New Hargeisa's respondents offer insights into the everyday choices shaping low-level policing, and the commonalities they share with Waberi's residents. The composition of the groups also provides a snapshot of the social environment in which 'the SLPF conducts its business, representing a cross-section of the age, education and marital status of residents in Macalin Haaruun and its surrounding districts. Its clan and gender composition, educational attainments and experience of government are different from Waberi, yet people's expectations of police–community relations are not fundamentally dissimilar, while the officers concerned appear to share functional and attitudinal commonalities with their peers in Mogadishu. New Hargeisa's residents are generally satisfied with the police and – this is key – wish to support officers, arranging their lives to accommodate the police's limited resources and reactive role. Most recognise, and use, the police station as their preferred site for engagement, even if few use their visit to report crime. Indeed, few claimed to report crime to police, with elders playing a mediating role between the two. With the exception of low-key collaborative efforts to ensure that some form of night-time policing is available, neither residents nor the police seek to change current patterns of engagement. And neither regards ICT as desirable.

Conclusions

New Hargeisa's experience of the text alert experiment offers insight into the potential connection between technology and police–community relations that donors, although not residents, hope will improve police–community engagement. More importantly, it illustrates the everyday choices shaping low-level policing and community safety while showing how local norms and preferences can negate the availability of a globalised technology; high rates of access to mobiles does not necessarily improve communications – or trust – between police and residents. People may have access to mobiles but they choose not to send text alert messages even though officers have (in theory) the manpower, mobiles, radios, vehicles and training needed to respond to daytime calls.

Meanwhile, the SLPF's response to both ICT and community engagement is casual. In December 2015, one senior officer said that the text alert system worked well in New Hargeisa, although not necessarily elsewhere in the city, whereas his colleague said that the text alert system did not work anywhere because people did not understand it.[30]

The reasons for this are debatable, but education and publicity campaigns are unlikely to make a significant difference to the assessment of either the police or residents because officers already have the knowledge and skills needed to fulfil societal expectations regarding the management of low-level insecurity, while residents' responses help to reproduce the police responses so often criticised. In all cases, police stations remain the preferred site for engagement; one-to-one communication between officers and residents is more important than international-style community policing. Senior officers ask donors for more advice, training and equipment to improve engagement, but then fail to use what they have, while the exploitation of even basic technology may prove too challenging for Macalin Haaruun's barely educated police, most of whom are unfamiliar with either keyboard skills or in displaying initiative. At the same time, Hargeisa's oral society ignores publicity campaigns by the Ministry of Interior, preferring to report issues to the police verbally (by mobile calls if necessary) or on paper. In Hargeisa, as in Mogadishu, the response is essentially the affirmation of local preferences, and ICT has little or no impact on police–community engagement.

---

[30] Author interview with senior officers, Hargeisa, 8 December 2015.

CONCLUSIONS

Unlike most analyses of Mogadishu's security governance, which concentrate on high-level developments involving the international community's plans for Somalia's stabilisation and political progress, this Whitehall Paper explores the ways in which the city's Somali inhabitants assess street-level threats and try to mitigate insecurity. It uses Mogadishu's city security plan and its constituent parts – most notably, the Waberi district neighbourhood-watch scheme – as an entrance into the city's security dynamics. This enables a consideration of issues such as the connections between counterterrorism and community safety, the contribution of community cohesion and mobilisation to sustainable civilian policing, and the potential of ICT to improve the police–community engagement on which state- and capacity-building is thought to depend. In other words, the city security plan and neighbourhood-watch scheme allow for a concrete conceptualisation of problems and problem-solving that help to generate insights into the nature of (in)security in an otherwise inaccessible environment. They also allow an exploration of the interface between three issues usually kept separate: hard and soft security; formal and informal policing provision; and international and local perspectives on security. The result is a more balanced picture of the city's security provision.

Mogadishu's security environment is shaped by terrorist, insurgent, criminal and militia networks entrenched in clan identity politics, all of which are exacerbated by chronic violence, poverty, deprivation, inequality and alienation. Although security is formally the responsibility of the FGS, the Benadir Regional Administration, the SPF and NISA, most people rely on informal providers, such as local clan- and district-based militia. However, sharply distinguishing between formal and informal provision is misleading because the borders between the two are porous and shift according to need. Thus, the city security plan draws on information collected by illiterate women who rely on clan-based protection, but choose to visit police stations to discuss their concerns, while the police force operates between the city security plan's structure and neighbourhood-watch schemes, and militiamen wear police uniforms.

One reason for this is because counterterrorism and community welfare form part of a coherent whole based on everyone's need for physical security. Nevertheless, Mogadishu's security governance is dominated by its need to counter terrorism, and the central issue confronting the FGS, the regional administration and residents is how best to reduce the insecurity and vulnerability associated with Al-Shabaab. The government is dysfunctional, the regional administration is driven by mayoral politics, the police's role is minimal, and residents have few resources beyond clan affiliation. In the circumstances, neighbourhood-watch schemes offer a proven, sustainable and locally acceptable way to collect and structure information and intelligence. Further, public information is a strategic resource and, in collecting information, neighbourhood-watch schemes help to provide the actionable intelligence the JIMC needs to dislocate terrorist networks. It encourages social cohesion and mobilisation while connecting households to the city's security plan.

Neighbourhood-watch schemes also have the potential to improve the reporting and prevention of everyday crime and thus facilitate a locally appropriate form of community policing, while helping to reduce street-level insecurity. But this is not their primary purpose. Similarly, the SPF may occasionally respond to street crime, but its role is to collect intelligence and act as a filter between neighbourhood-watch schemes and the joint intelligence and operations management centres, rather than to provide community reassurance or partnership policing. As ever, the style of policing found in the districts depends on the area commander; Waberi's is supportive of neighbourhood watch and police–community engagement, as is the regional administration's commissioner, but many senior and mid-ranking officers are not, and few if any general-duty officers know or care about any form of community-oriented policing.

In practice, preventing crime relies on residents taking responsibility for their own safety, security and property. Further, most police and residents do not communicate with each other, and the presence of Al-Shabaab and its sympathisers means that many people fear to be seen with the police. Nevertheless, better communications could improve police–community relations, making policing easier and the streets safer for both officers and residents. Hence, commentators inspired by Kenya's experience argue that the use of ICT will help to shift attitudes and to facilitate the cultural change needed for meaningful police–community engagement. But international models of community policing lack traction, while basic and more inclusive forms of ICT play a bigger part in policing initiatives than mobiles or crisis lines. Significantly, Hargeisa's experience is similar, suggesting that local norms and preferences can counteract the use of globalised technology.

Based on Mogadishu's experience, answers to the three questions posed in the Introduction are as follows:

1. What is the most sustainable way to collect the intelligence needed to make Mogadishu's residents safe?

Neighbourhood-watch schemes are the most cost-effective, structured, sustainable and locally acceptable way to collect the information and actionable intelligence needed to make Mogadishu's streets safe in the face of terrorist attacks and crimes such as property theft and abduction. It is not known how the authorities or residents accommodate or anticipate gaps and uncertainties in the knowledge needed to achieve this, but both will have developed their own security guidelines and anticipatory knowledge – they would not otherwise survive.

2. What is known about the relationship between counterterrorism and community safety in Mogadishu?

Mogadishu's authorities and residents understand its security situation as comprising or representing a coherent and comprehensive picture in which a range of actors and mutually reinforcing issues are integrated into a meaningful whole. Admittedly, most security actors focus only on clan-related concerns. Nevertheless, this broad-based understanding of security suggests that the sharp categorisations found in Western literature lack relevance. For example, the boundaries between counterterrorism and community safety are more permeable and relative to time and place than Western experience and analysis suggests, and the points of interface are more informal and numerous. Similarly, distinctions between 'hard' and 'soft security' mean little when the threat of physical coercion underpins many aspects of daily life: police officers prize weaponry and rapid-response skills over community policing; women IDPs are subject to high rates of rape and domestic violence; and journalists and NGO activists are frequently threatened. In the same way, distinctions between state and non-state actors and processes amount to little when the Somali state is essentially the FGS, which is reliant on its international supporters even as it pursues an entrepreneurial agenda based on identity politics. It is probable that comparable observations apply to security and stability and the tipping points between them; it could not be otherwise after several decades of conflict.

3. To what extent can ICT help to improve the police–community engagement on which sustainable forms of low-level security depend?

For now, mobiles play no part in crime-reporting or police response rates. Although many of Mogadishu's residents have access to mobile phones, police stations remain their preferred site for engagement, just as they do in Hargeisa. In Mogadishu, as in Hargeisa, local norms and preferences counteract the availability of international ideals and policing models and globalised technology. The potential for ICT to shape the location, demands and results of police–community engagement is consequently minimal; access to ICT does not necessarily lead to responsive or accountable policing.

Mogadishu is safer now than it has been for several decades, yet its experience suggests that security provision and policing are essentially negative, and are about minimising insecurity and avoiding danger, rather than service, partnership or community policing. The ability or desire of the SPF to change this situation is minimal, for policing has been selectively constituted in the light of legacy issues, contingencies and political goals, with security levels, political settlements, technical resources, personal experience, pragmatism and international influence acting as critical variables. In other words, policing consolidates security practices. And residents in districts such as Waberi and Macalin Haaruun accept this. Nevertheless, some choose to support their local officers, arranging their lives to accommodate the police's limited resources and reactive role, just as they do with the FGS and regional administration. From this perspective, the key to understanding police–community engagement and sustainable policing models is in the knowledge, skills and tactical flexibility officers and residents need to fulfil societal, rather than international, expectations.

Ultimately, in fragmented and violent cities such as Mogadishu, security reflects the sum of many local arrangements and is best understood as a coherent, comprehensive and relational concept rooted in the need for physical security now, rather than in the future.

About Whitehall Papers

The Whitehall Paper series provides in-depth studies of specific developments, issues or themes in the field of national and international defence and security. Three Whitehall Papers are published each year. They reflect the highest standards of original research and analysis, and are invaluable background material for specialists and policymakers alike.

About RUSI

The Royal United Services Institute (RUSI) is the world's oldest and the UK's leading defence and security think tank. Its mission is to inform, influence and enhance public debate on a safer and more stable world. RUSI is a research-led institute, producing independent, practical and innovative analysis to address today's complex challenges.

Since its foundation in 1831, RUSI has relied on its members to support its activities. Together with revenue from research, publications and conferences, RUSI has sustained its political independence for more than 185 years.